Buffalo!

Buffalo!

by

Craig Boddington

SAFARI PRESS

The trademark Safari Press ® is registered with the U.S. Patent and Trademark Office and in other countries.

Boddington, Craig

Second edition

Safari Press Inc.

2006, Long Beach, California

ISBN 1-57157-354-2

Library of Congress Catalog Card Number: 2005926481

10 9 8 7 6 5 4 3 2

Readers wishing to receive the Safari Press catalog, featuring many fine books on big-game hunting, wingshooting, and sporting firearms, should write to Safari Press Inc., P.O. Box 3095, Long Beach, CA 90803, USA. Tel: (714) 894-9080 or visit our Web site at www.safaripress.com.

Dedication

To the great professional hunters and trackers who have led me on the spoor and taught me so much. At the start, I was much younger than they and badly needed their guidance. Today, I am often much older ... and I still have so much to learn from them.

Table of Contents

This is a good bull, which I took with Andrew Dawson in the Zambezi Valley in 2004. This one is exactly 40 inches wide, old and heavy-horned, a great trophy. Buffalo bulls vary considerably in body size, but I have seen few as large as this one. He won't weigh a ton, but he's probably pushing 1,800 pounds.

Why Hunt Buffalo?
Chapter 1

We had spent the morning hunting on foot, high on the slopes of Mount Kenya, where the tall forest of ancient trees gave way to bamboo. We had seen little and were headed back down, following a finger of clear, green meadow between the trees. A steep-sided waterway cut laterally across the meadow, unseen until we almost stepped into it. Cool mud lined the bottom, and in that cool mud wallowed the first Cape buffalo bull I'd ever seen. He came out literally under our feet, scrambled up the far bank, then turned and faced us at just a few yards.

Robert Ruark wrote that the Cape buffalo "looks at you like you owe him money." Nobody ever said it better, neither in a century of great African writing before Ruark, nor in the half century since. I doubt anyone ever will, and I'm not going to try: That buffalo looked at me like I owed him a *lot* of money! He was coal black and covered with glistening mud. An old bull, his heavy helmet of a boss was corrugated and nearly grown together in the center. The horns were well formed, but narrow. My rifle had come up before he cleared the top of the far bank, but professional hunter Willem van Dyk stayed me with a hand on my arm. "Let him go," he said. "We'll do better."

So we stared each other down for several more seconds, that first buffalo and I. Then he turned and trotted out of the meadow and into the tall trees. I can honestly say that I wasn't frightened despite all the reading I'd done that described buffalo with words such as "vindictive," "aggressive," "fearsome," and worse. But he had my undivided attention and my utmost respect. Whether I feared him or not, it was clear that he didn't

Nobody said it better than Robert Ruark, when he wrote that a buffalo "looks at you like you owe him money." This is an exceptionally good bull, and whatever I owe him, I'm willing to pay!

fear me! I stood there with my PH a while longer, wishing that his horns were just a wee bit bigger, and I looked forward to further encounters with his kind.

That was twenty-seven years ago, and there have been many encounters with buffalo since then. On that cool, well-remembered morning in Kenya, I did not imagine that I would be so incredibly fortunate to have hunted in Africa as much as I have. As I look back, I'm somewhat bemused that my life has taken such a course. Or, perhaps better put, that I have driven my life along such a path. As I have written before, my intent on that first safari was to get Africa out of my system once and for all. Its result was the opposite: I have been smitten by Africa and her wildlife ever since, and I have returned every chance I've had.

In truth, I love it all. There are quite a few out-of-the-way corners I still hope to penetrate, and there are many places I would like to see "just one more time." To me, hunts are best remembered and trophies most appreciated when serious effort, whether mental, physical, or both, was expended, so I have a great fondness for Africa's more difficult prizes. These would include all the spiral-horned antelope; both great cats, the lion and the leopard; certainly elephant; and a few others that come to mind. If I can swing it, I will probably spend time on future safaris in all these pursuits. Regardless, one thing I know for certain: I will never tire of hunting buffalo.

My feelings toward them have changed little since that first meeting. In a close encounter, I am absolutely afraid of lions, and after one close brush with a wounded leopard, I can assure you that anyone who isn't very afraid under the same circumstances has something wrong upstairs. Cow elephant herds in thick cover are also the stuff of which nightmares are made. Perhaps oddly, though I don't think insanely, I have never been afraid of buffalo—although a couple of scary follow-ups have made my palms sweat and my knees a bit weak! Rather than fear, however, I approach them with caution and a respect that has only grown over the years.

To me, the African buffalo is the ultimate game animal. He is incredibly strong and wonderfully wary, armed with the full array of keen senses: Good eyes, keen hearing, and a wonderfully

Looking for buffalo tracks in a clearing far up on Mount Kenya, elevation something over ten thousand feet. It was in a clearing just like this that I had my first, close-up encounter with a Cape buffalo—and I'll never forget it.

There he is! Is he big enough? Am I close enough? Can I place the shot where I must? The adrenaline is pumping now, and it just doesn't get any better.

sensitive nose. He is also armed with sharp horns, his armored boss, and perhaps three-quarters of a ton of locomotive power, all backed by the skill and, sometimes, the will to use them all. This, to me, is what places him in a different class from a deer or an elk or a kudu, all of which have at least equal escape and evasion abilities. The buffalo has the capability to turn the tables!

Of course, the same can be said of the cats and elephant, and they are, indeed, fascinating and formidable game. But as game animals, there are differences. Unlike the cats, which I believe are very difficult to justify hunting over and over again, the buffalo yields a bountiful supply of tasty meat; he will always be fully utilized. This is also true of elephant, but here in the twenty-first century, there's a certain reality regarding them that must be recognized: While elephant are definitely overpopulated in many areas, the sheer costs of hunting them are such that very few of us can afford the experience even once, let alone multiple times.

Of the animals we call Africa's Big Five—the lion, leopard, buffalo, elephant, and rhino—the buffalo is far and away the most numerous and most available for hunting. He is also the most affordable. Buffalo hunting is no longer the great bargain that it was just twenty years ago (what is?), but buffalo remain available on relatively short hunts that are within the financial reach of those who want to hunt them badly enough.

It is extremely unlikely that I will ever shoot another rhino. I will almost certainly hunt leopard again, and if I can possibly find a way to afford it, I would like to hunt lion and elephant just once more. But I will almost certainly return to Africa to hunt buffalo—perhaps many more times. In large part, this is not only because I consider the buffalo such a wonderful game animal. It is also because they offer one of the greatest hunting experiences in the world.

The only way to hunt buffalo is to do so properly, on foot. If you do this, you will garner a lifetime's worth of memories—and if you do it repeatedly, you will only add to the treasure. Hunting buffalo is a classic piece of Africana, unchanged since the beginning of safari. You will find the tracks, and you will follow them wherever they lead. Sometimes you will catch up to the buffalo, and sometimes you won't, but you will see the magic of great African trackers pursuing their craft. Often you will catch

Art Wheaton and I pose with a nicely shaped, but very average, buffalo. So long as the bull is mature, size doesn't matter nearly as much as it does with some animals. What matters is hunting him right, on foot and face to face.

Looking for fresh buffalo spoor in the gorge of the Chewore River, in Zimbabwe's Zambezi Valley. Buffalo hunting can be as physical as you wish to make it, but most of the time there is a lot of walking involved.

up, but you will fail to get a shot. Then you will do it again, sweating through miles on the spoor and sweating more on the seemingly endless miles back to the truck. Sooner or later, with just a wee bit of luck, you will get a shot at your great, black, buffalo bull.

Although I have never been a record-book hunter, many animals need to be of a certain quality standard to be worthy. I do not feel this way about buffalo. A bull must be fully mature, with a good, hard boss, in order to be a trophy, but beyond that it really doesn't matter. The experience is all the same, and with buffalo, it's the experience, the close encounter and the moment of truth, that matter. It is true that I have spent much time searching for really big buffalo (not always with success), but this is more by way of stretching out the experience than because mine must be bigger than anyone else's. I don't believe in shooting young bulls, because they need a chance to grow up and breed; however, in some areas, cow buffalo are on license, usually at a much-reduced cost from bulls. The experience is absolutely equal, and the "trophy" selection much the same as you comb the herds for a particularly wide-horned cow.

Not all the African hunters I know are as silly over buffalo hunting as I am, but most continue to hunt buffalo on successive safaris. Among all my acquaintances who have hunted Africa, I know just one man who has taken exactly one buffalo and has no desire to ever take another. I've always been too polite to ask, but my suspicion is that they came across a herd either crossing or alongside a road and his professional hunter allowed (or coerced) him into shooting a bull from the vehicle. Buffalo are wary enough that the opportunity to actually do this is rare, but it does happen, and it is legal in some areas. I feel sorry for the unsuspecting client who does this, and, legal or not, I have absolutely no respect for any professional hunter who would allow an able-bodied client to shoot a buffalo from a vehicle. The client, often new to Africa and not knowing any better, has been cheated out of the great experience of a real buffalo hunt. He can never have the memories he should have every time he looks at his mounted trophy, regardless of the size of the bull.

Over the years, I have had very few opportunities to be tempted by such a scenario, and I can honestly say I have never

None of these three bulls was quite what we were looking for, so we let them go. But that doesn't matter at all. What does matter is getting close to buffalo, and no other experience can match it.

Dave and Janice Fulson with Janice's first buffalo. Unlike so many game animals, a buffalo doesn't have to be huge to be a wonderful trophy. Buffalo hunting is really all about the experience. (Photo by Dave Fulson)

shot one even in proximity to a vehicle. Most of the buffalo I've seen from a road have been fading into the brush. The easy solution is to simply let them get completely out of sight, then get the wind right and proceed on foot. This I have done many times. But, once in a while a great bull will stand flatfooted and look at you. This happened to my buddy Cameron Hopkins in Tanzania. Apparently, it was a great bull, far better than any he has ever taken to this day. He refused to shoot, which, as the scene developed, turned into a resolute and courageous stand. His professional hunter was so furious that, after the bull finally turned and crashed off into the brush, he refused to follow and didn't speak for the rest of the day. I don't think there are many so-called professional hunters in Africa who would behave in this fashion, but when you plan a buffalo hunt, tell your PH that you want to *hunt* buffalo. You'll be glad you did!

Elsewhere in this book, we will deal specifically with the subject of following wounded buffalo and the inherent perils of this activity. Right now, up front, as it were, I want to touch on the raw danger of hunting buffalo, or at least my opinion of it. Again, I have the utmost respect for buffalo and am always cautious around them. That said, I sincerely believe buffalo are rarely dangerous unless serious mistakes are made, usually in shot placement or follow-up. Unprovoked charges are truly extremely rare, and I have never seen anything close to such an event.

This doesn't mean bad things can't happen. In 2004, just a few months ago as I write these lines, a buffalo in Tanzania's Masailand killed Bob Fontana, a great British Columbia outfitter. He and his professional hunter—who is a very good friend of mine and a really fine PH—went into some cover early one morning, looking for a big lesser kudu they had glimpsed earlier in the hunt. A buffalo came out of nowhere and killed Fontana almost instantly. The buffalo apparently took a bullet, but was neither stopped nor recovered, so why the buffalo attacked is anybody's guess.

In 2000, when we were hunting in the Selous Reserve, my old buddy Chub Eastman took an absolutely unprovoked charge. Chub had one leg in a cast, hip to toe, from a recent motorcycle crash (this was one of those situations when shooting from a vehicle is just fine!). The trackers actually *carried* him on several stalks, and he got his buffalo on foot (just not *his* feet). Except for this one. Chub was in the open truck bed, his PH negotiating the Land Cruiser around a big termite mound, when a buffalo bull launched a charge from very close range, headed like a torpedo aimed straight amidships and right toward the PH, who had taken the doors off the truck. Somehow or other, Chub managed to grab his .375 and spine the beast from above; it slid forward as it crashed until its nose was almost under the truck.

As I said, charges usually result from mistakes—but the mistakes don't have to be your own. In the case of the buffalo that killed Fontana we will never know, but chances are pretty good that it was carrying a poacher's bullet, had caught a foot in a snare, had a close brush with a lion, or perhaps had simply lost a fight with another bull and had an attitude. As rare as unprovoked charges are, it is almost inconceivable for one to come from a perfectly healthy animal. In Eastman's case, this bull had a really nasty, festering wound high on the inside of a hind leg. It could have been from a horn, or it could have been from some strange accident out in the bush, but this animal was clearly suffering and was probably mad at the world.

Provoked charges are far more common, though still relatively rare; but that depends a lot on how bad you screw up. In July of 2004, I was sitting around a camp in the Sapi concession of the Zambezi Valley, surrounded by a bunch of really experienced hunters—professional hunters Andrew Dawson and Paul Smith; Tim Danklef and Dave Fulson, producers of the *Boddington on Buffalo* film; and Richard Harland, also a professional hunter and a truly legendary Zimbabwe hunter with incredible experience. With experience around that fire into the many hundreds of buffalo, we were trying to put a number on how many wounded buffalo will actually charge: It *is* absolutely true that a wounded buffalo will lie in ambush for his tormentors, at least sometimes. No one can say, but our consensus was that it's something like one in ten.

We did note that the first mistake, poor shot placement, had already been made. What happens from there depends on a lot of things: How thick the brush, how serious the wound, the individual character of that buffalo, and, perhaps above all, how careful the follow-up. It is quite possible to increase that percentage of charges by following carelessly, by failing to shoot or only further wounding when the wounded bull is again sighted, or by approaching a downed but not dead animal so as to allow the buffalo to see you. I have no patience with this. Enough mistakes will be made without making them on purpose.

Buffalo are dangerous, and people can get hurt. It's as simple as that. On the other hand, I think the buffalo gets a bad rap, to some degree. All he really wants to do is graze, chew his cud, roll in mud, drink water, and breed, resting peacefully in the shade when he's had his fill of all these things. I can hardly blame a wounded buffalo that lies in wait for something that has hurt him, and he is certainly cunning enough to do that. But he is not demonic, he is not normally "vindictive," and under most circumstances, he is not even aggressive. Ah, but he has the capability, and that makes him magnificent! He requires hard, serious hunting, on his own turf and terms. He is incredibly strong, requiring powerful rifles and good bullets to bring him down, and he deserves to be taken with well-placed shots. Some writers have called him ugly, but I will not. With his heavy boss and the graceful sweep of his horns, I think he is beautiful, and I hope I get to hunt his tribe many more times.

Africa's Cape Buffalo
Chapter 2

There are several races of African buffalo, species *Syncerus caffer*, but the one most often referred to is the southern, or Cape, buffalo. He is the largest in both body and horn. He is also the most numerous and widespread, occurring across a huge chunk of the continent, north to south from Kenya to South Africa, and in southern Africa, east to west from Mozambique to Angola.

He is not continuous throughout this vast range; buffalo are extremely adaptable animals, but they must have water. I've hunted them in swampy country in the Okavango and Bangweulu, in the forests far up on Mount Kenya, and in more typical thornbush, mopane forest, and *miombo* forest in a half-dozen countries. Common to all is water. I've followed herds that, by the tracks, seemed to have skipped a day, but generally speaking, they must have the resource daily. So you won't find buffalo in Africa's great deserts, but, naturally, at one time they occurred almost everywhere else.

Man changed that. Buffalo carry a number of bovine diseases that can be transmitted to cattle, so during the last two centuries, buffalo have been eradicated from vast areas to make room for livestock. In some areas, this process continues to this day, but in others, the pendulum has swung back. Back in the late 1970s, I was one of the first sportsmen to hunt on Roger Whittall's Humani Ranch in the southeastern lowveld, in the Sabi River valley. Only a couple of years earlier, Roger had finally "beaten" the buffalo problem. Then, with the long Rhodesian bush war starting to wind down, he decided to go into the safari business.

Buffalo are herd animals, and in areas where the animals are plentiful, herds can run to 500 or more. This massive herd was photographed on the flood plains in Botswana's Chobe region. (Photograph by Debra Bradbury)

Of course, I wanted to hunt buffalo, but after years of intensive shooting to make way for cattle, there were only a few incredibly spooky survivors along the Sabi.

Twenty years passed, and the wildlife business was still good. Roger and his neighbors got together and formed the Sabi Valley Conservancy and, at great cost, brought back the buffalo. I didn't get one "way back then," but, in 1996, I shot a nice bull out of a healthy, undisturbed herd.

Buffalo have been reintroduced on several private conservancies in Zimbabwe, but their neighbors to the south have encountered problems with their efforts to do the same. South Africa has a huge game-ranching industry, with as many as nine thousand game ranches in that country alone. Many are neither large enough for buffalo nor have suitable habitat—but many are ideal. The problem in South Africa is that buffalo reintroduced into ranch country (much of which is former buffalo range), must be certified disease-free. Most "clean" buffalo herds have their origins from remnant herds in the almost impenetrable Addo bush not far from Port Elizabeth, those herds separated from all other buffalo populations for generations. Availability of breeding stock for reintroduction is very limited, and the prices are frightful. Buffalo are fairly prolific, and it doesn't take long for herds to expand exponentially, but that, of course, depends on the size of the "starter herd." There is also ongoing experimentation in breeding programs that may, over time, expedite things.

Over time, I predict we will see a lot more buffalo in South Africa. But it takes a long time—about a decade—to grow a trophy bull. So, for the time being, unlike so many antelope species, the best hunting opportunities are found in natural populations. The good news is that although the Cape buffalo's range has shrunk dramatically from what it once was, there are still plenty of animals. No one really knows how many, but they still roam across East and southern Africa in many hundreds of thousands.

A really wide-horned cow taken by Mike Campos in an area where buffalo cows were on license. Cow buffalo can grow huge horns; the primary difference between bulls and cows is that females have absolutely no boss. (Photo by Dave Fulson)

Thanks to the great demand for buffalo among international sportsmen, game ranchers in southern Africa have reintroduced buffalo into many areas where buffalo were eradicated to make way for livestock. In both South Africa and Namibia, the critical issue is the supply of disease-free breeding stock. (Photo by Dave Fulson)

The Great Black Buffalo

In the north, he is most often called *mbogo*, his Swahili name. In southern Africa, he is most often called *nyati*, probably Zulu in origin, but common to several languages. His English name, Cape buffalo, is taken from South Africa's Cape of Good Hope, where Europeans first encountered him. By any name, he is a lot of bull! I have often read that Cape buffalo "weigh a ton." The problem is that very few people have ever actually weighed Cape buffalo in the wild. I'm not one of them, but I don't believe many (if any) Cape buffalo bulls ever weigh a full two thousand pounds.

They vary a lot, but I reckon something like fifteen hundred pounds, three-fourths of a ton, is a very normal weight for a big-bodied, mature bull. Some get larger. The SCI book suggests fourteen hundred to eighteen hundred pounds, and I concur, 100 percent. I shot a big old bull in the Zambezi Valley, in 2004, and I think he was the biggest-bodied buffalo I have ever shot. I don't know what he weighed—not a ton—but he might have been close.

On the other hand, some buffalo seem a bit smaller. I've taken quite a few bulls in Tanzania's Selous Reserve. Most of them, like the Selous elephants, have seemed to me to be a fair amount smaller than the average Zimbabwe bull.

But that's all hair splitting. Whether he weighs fourteen hundred pounds or eighteen hundred pounds, he's still a lot of bull! The Cape buffalo is a blocky, strongly built animal with huge shoulders, thick chest, powerful neck, and sturdy legs. Pound for pound he is incredibly strong, and he seems able to command a vast surge of adrenaline. Perhaps this is because, in most buffalo areas, in order to grow old, he must fend off lions all his life. And despite the horror stories, Cape buffalo are not bulletproof at all. They can be killed very readily with a single, well-placed shot. Ah, but if that first shot isn't well placed, all bets are off! Once he gets the adrenaline going, he can seem almost impossible to put down.

Immature animals, and even the occasional mature cow, are more brownish than black. But southern buffalo are

Poling through the reeds in a dugout canoe is an unusual way to hunt buffalo, but it works—sometimes all too well.

The defining characteristic of a buffalo bull is his boss—a hard, helmetlike horn that on a mature bull appears as if the two horns have grown together. This bull, taken by PH Andrew Dawson and hunter Mike Campos, is not wide, but has a super boss and deep curl and is fully mature. In my view, and that of most experienced, professional hunters, this is what you're looking for.

predominantly black, and I have never seen a mature southern bull that was anything else. This is one of several differences between *Syncerus caffer caffer*, the southern or Cape buffalo, and the northern and western races. With Nile buffalo, one starts to see brownish and reddish animals within the herd. As you move west, this becomes more and more prevalent; the dwarf forest buffalo, *S. c. nanus*, is universally red. The black coloring, by the way, is just hair. Underneath, the skin is predominantly gray. The length of that black hair varies considerably. Some older bulls are downright bald, at least in patches, and thus look very gray. Other buffalo have a uniform coating of stiff black hair and look extremely black. Not too surprisingly, at least in my experience, the coats tend to be a bit more luxuriant in cooler areas.

That being said, I don't know anyone who has hunted buffalo for the quality of his cape! Southern buffalo have, by far, the largest horns, and they are spectacular. Note that I said "buffalo," not "bulls." Both sexes have horns, and buffalo cows can, and sometimes do, grow incredible horns. In fact, some of the widest-horned buffalo known have been cows, not bulls. In Zambia, in 1984, Russ Broom and I spent an entire afternoon working a huge herd of buffalo. Lord, there must have been more than five hundred. There was one huge cow that we must have seen a half-dozen times, once from an ant heap at no more than twenty yards. Her horns dropped way down and swept out forever—she must have had a spread of at least fifty inches!

During one's first few experiences with buffalo, it can be very, very difficult to tell the bulls from the cows, but the signs are fairly clear once you know what to look for. Bulls are generally larger in the body, though not always. In short grass, the bull's penis sheath will be obvious. After you've looked at a few bulls, so will his deep masculine neck and massive shoulders. Cows are simply not as powerfully built, ever.

Most important, however, is the boss. Cow horns develop more from the side of the head than from the top, and the forehead will always be covered with at least a sparse covering of hair. A young bull may look much the same, but that's OK because you aren't looking for a young bull. A mature bull will have developed that thick, helmetlike growth of horn that we call the "boss." It takes at least seven or eight years for that boss to develop fully, and even then, the inner edges will likely be soft and lightly covered with hair. By the age of nine, perhaps ten, the boss will be completely formed into hard horn. The inner edges will usually be close together, often so close that only a thin line distinguishes one horn from the other.

It is probably at this point that a bull's horns will be at their very best, fully formed and with sharp tips. If not taken by a lion or a bullet, a Cape buffalo in the wild might live fifteen or sixteen years, depending on tooth wear, but in later years, horn wear will outpace horn growth. His tips will wear down or break off, and once in a while you will encounter an ancient old, outcast bull that has no horns at all, only the football-helmet covering of his boss.

Bosses vary considerably. Some are much wider than others, and some buffalo bulls will always have a gap of a couple of inches between the horns. Whatever, the issue is that the boss be comprised of fully hard horn, and for most serious buffalo hunters, this is the defining mark of a completely mature and, thus, shootable bull.

The boss is, of course, just one aspect of a buffalo's horns. Just like mule deer hunters speak in terms of spread, the most commonly quoted feature of a buffalo's horns is the outside spread. A decent, average, mature bull will have a spread of something like thirty-six to thirty-eight inches. Always and forever, forty is considered very good. Up into the mid-forties is fabulous, and hunters speak in hushed tones of the very few buffalo that have reached fifty inches. Perhaps more important than spread, though, is the configuration of the horns. Ideally, you want the horns to drop well down and then curve into the tips in a beautiful arc. A very wide bull may have extremely flat horns that simply come straight out and are not attractive at all; a somewhat narrower bull with a deep curve may be both more beautiful and more impressive. And a bull that has a very wide spread and perfect configuration—but still has soft, hair-covered bosses—is not a trophy at all. I'll discuss this in greater detail later on.

Back at the skinning shed with a buffalo carcass. Absent refrigeration, meat that cannot be quickly utilized will be cut into thin strips and dried as biltong, *African jerky.*

Buffalo have wide, sensitive ears covered with soft hair on the inner surfaces. There is nothing at all wrong with these ears. When buffalo are moving and feeding, you have a wee bit of latitude, but when they're resting, all senses are on high alert, and a careless footstep will be the end of that stalk. The eyes are black and fairly keen. I do not think they see nearly as well as some of the antelope species—or perhaps don't place as much reliance on their vision—but, when stalking a herd slowly and carefully and with good cover, I have often been amazed at the distances at which a watchful cow will suddenly fix all her attention on me. Like most game animals, however, the buffalo's shotgun-muzzle nose is the first line of defense. You might get away with snapping a dry twig, and, if you're careful, stealthy movement is possible, at least to within shooting range. But one whiff of human scent, and the jig is up. It doesn't take much, just a puff of swirling breeze.

Typically, unless they have a place they must get to, buffalo will move more or less into the wind so that they know what's in front of them. They might continue to move this way when spooked once, but you won't push them more than a time or two before they'll move with a following wind. Then, it's all over for that day. Of course, this is a typical tactic for a wounded buffalo—except that he won't always run away!

Habits and Habitat

Buffalo are primarily a grazing ruminant. They will also browse their way along, but grass is their staple diet. This means that they must come into relatively open country to graze, but they prefer heavy cover for daytime resting. Let's start their day at noon, in the thickest, nastiest cover available in the area.

They will rest there through the heat of the day, spread out, lying down, chewing their cuds some of the time and sleeping intermittently, but always with some buffalo paying attention. They will normally get up late in the afternoon, perhaps two hours before dusk, and begin grazing their way along. Depending on where their shady cover is in relation to good grazing and water (and also depending on the moonlight), they may water in

Buffalo need water almost every day, usually coming to water some time between late afternoon and early morning.

the early evening, during the night, or first thing in the morning. They will graze through the night, but they will also spend some of this time resting and ruminating. Their night vision is just fine, but I don't believe they generally move great distances at night. Certainly they feel secure at night, provided lions leave them alone, and will often spend several nighttime hours resting in open country.

In the early morning, they do the reverse, feeding their way slowly back into heavy cover. They are not on any schedule, but they don't move much during the heat of the day. Usually they will reach bedding cover and lie down by about eleven o'clock, but I have noticed that during a full moon, they are likely to lie down earlier. This suggests that they move and feed more on moonlit nights, which shouldn't come as rocket science.

They are fairly random in their movements. They might stay in an area with really good grass for a few days, and they will often water at the same point for successive days, but this depends a lot on how many options are available. Lions will move them around, and, of course, we hunters do, but their movements are

When I first hunted on Roger Whittall's Humani Ranch in the '70s, buffalo were almost gone, eradicated over concerns about hoof-and-mouth disease. Twenty years later, after much effort, the buffalo were back, and I finally got one along Zimbabwe's Sabi River. This, by the way, is the only "freak" buffalo I have ever taken, with a right horn like an upside down eland horn.

primarily dictated by grass, water, and security cover. Depending on these and their own bovine whims, they may move several miles in the course of a night's feeding—or only a few hundred yards. Many cattle ranchers around the world, including my part of central California, regard Zimbabwean Alan Savory as a guru in livestock range management. His theories on rotational grazing, what he calls "holistic range management," are based on his observations of the effect of the random movement of Cape buffalo herds on the bushveld of his native land.

They are herd animals, mostly. A mixed herd of cows and calves may have as few as a dozen or twenty animals, or as many as five hundred and more. If there is an average size, then I think it depends on the local population. Obviously, if you keep running into big herds in the hundreds, then there are lots and lots of buffalo in that area! I tend to think that herds of maybe sixty or so are fairly normal. Most mixed herds will have some bulls, often trailing the herd. You often hear references to *dugga* (also spelled *dagga*), bulls. *Dugga* is a word in several African languages, though most familiarly Shona, for "mud." Buffalo love to wallow in mud, and bulls are often covered with the stuff. A "*dugga* boy," however, is considered to be a mature bachelor bull, scabby and balding, often with worn-down horns.

This is all misleading, as the herd dynamics come and go. Most of the bulls within a mixed herd will be young bulls and breeding age bulls, maybe up to ten years old. Bulls will break off into bachelor herds, away from the wives and kids, and you might find bulls of all ages in a bachelor group of perhaps twenty, sometimes even more. True *dugga* boys will be older bulls that are mostly past breeding. They are the old-timers, much more likely to be found as single bulls or in the company of up to a half-dozen of their peers. However, excepting perhaps the really senile ones, *dugga* boys will also come and go within a herd. So you can't say that a herd of any size won't have a really good bull. Nor can you say that a bachelor group automatically will. These are subjects for later, more in-depth discussion.

Wherever buffalo are found, they are the primary and preferred prey of lions. Lions do occur where there are no buffalo, but in a natural setting, where you find buffalo in numbers, you will find lions. The lions take their share, but in a normal and healthy predator-to-prey ratio, the cats probably have little effect on the overall numbers. Disease *is* an issue. Several times in known history, devastating epidemics of bovine diseases, such as rinderpest, have swept through buffalo herds. This apparently happened not long before Theodore Roosevelt's 1909 safari, and although he took buffalo, he hunted hard for them and did not see anything like the numbers that might be seen in the same regions today.

Buffalo are actually quite slow breeders, so once the population reaches critical low numbers, it takes a very long time for them to come back. The breeding season is generally just after the end of the rainy season, around May, when the grass is at its best. Calves are born eleven months later. Under ideal conditions, a cow might produce a calf every year, but in Africa's continual bust-and-boom cycles of periodic drought, it's more likely that a cow will produce a single calf just every two to four years. This makes it a numbers game. If your area has ten thousand buffalo, a recruitment of as little as 25 percent is clearly more than enough to support plenty of lions and any sensible hunting program. But if you're starting from scratch with a nucleus herd, it takes a long time for a score of animals to build up to viable numbers.

In recent months, I've had several discussions with Kimberley Beck of RESCU International (Reproduction of Endangered Species of Captive Ungulates). Recognizing both the desirability of buffalo in South Africa's game-ranching scene and the dangerously small genetic pool of disease-free stock, her group has a project to enhance buffalo reproduction using assisted reproductive technologies fairly common to the cattle-ranching industry. Much of it is over my head, but with human populations and livestock increasing apace across so much of Africa, it is clearly essential to expand the availability of "clean" buffalo as rapidly as possible.

Buffalo Country

In the north, neither Kenya nor Uganda are currently hunted. At one time, Uganda had tremendous numbers of buffalo; into the 1970s, the standard hunting license allowed *five!* This country's wildlife was badly ravaged during Idi Amin's reign of terror, but there are almost certainly some pockets of buffalo here and there. Kenya, closed since 1977, was famous for big buffalo. But today, Kenya has a huge human population, and there is relatively little wildlife outside of her parks. Still, the big buffalo are there. In 1998, I spent several months in coastal Kenya on a military exercise. I didn't have much time to look around, but the local papers often mentioned incidents with crop-raiding elephant and buffalo. I did manage to spend a few days in Tsavo National Park, and I have never seen such a concentration of huge buffalo bulls as I did there. Undoubtedly, there are still plenty of monsters up on Mount Kenya and the other areas that have, historically, produced really big trophies. Technically, Uganda never closed hunting; it just faded away when

Idi Amin came to power. I believe there may be some limited hunting there again, perhaps by the time you read this, and there will almost certainly be some buffalo. After twenty-five years, I no longer believe Kenya will ever reopen—but man, after what I saw, what I'd give for a chance to hunt buffalo like that!

Today, when hunters think of big buffalo, Tanzania is the country most likely to come to mind. In a later chapter, I will dispute this. Tanzania has big buffalo, but it is not the only area that does, and, depending on time and place, may not be the best. But it is great buffalo country—almost all of it! Buffalo are well distributed throughout Tanzania's hunting areas, from Masailand down through the Rungwa region and off to the west. The concentration is truly incredible in the vast Selous Reserve. Tanzania's twenty-one day license still allows three buffalo, and even the seven-day license allows two. There are lots of buffalo in Tanzania, but bulls with horns spreading into the mid-forties and beyond aren't hiding behind every tree.

Geoff Broom and I are overlooking a flood plain on the Ugalla River, in western Tanzania. It isn't common to catch buffalo in such open country during daylight. They will more probably come out to feed at night, and they will leave tracks.

Mozambique once held vast numbers of buffalo, but their numbers were drastically reduced during the twenty-year bush war that only ended in the mid-1980s. There is still reasonable buffalo hunting in Mozambique, especially in her portion of the Zambezi Valley. The game is rebuilding, but it's coming back from a very low point, so I think it's fair to say that today we are still hunting remnant herds. It will get better, but it's going to take time.

In the past quarter-century, Malawi has been open to hunting only briefly (and abortively). There are certainly populations of buffalo here and there, but I don't see much potential. In 2004, veteran professional hunters George Angelides, Nicky Blunt, and Dougie Stephenson actually managed to get a hunting operation going in former Zaire, now the Democratic Republic of Congo (D.R.C.). In the northern forests, where they're concentrating their operations, the smaller forest buffalo coexist with bongo. But the southern provinces of this vast, little-known country are the areas that are almost certain to hold large numbers of Cape buffalo. At some point, these buffalo must transition to the smaller northern races, so trophy quality probably isn't fabulous. In any case, the logistical challenges of running a viable safari operation in this region are such that I doubt we'll ever know.

The D.R.C.'s southern neighbor, Zambia, is a whole different story. Formerly Northern Rhodesia, Zambia has been an important hunting country since the 1970s. Regrettably, hunting was closed for three seasons due to a politically charged and excruciatingly drawn-out "reallocation of areas," not reopening until 2003. Prior to the closure, Zambia was a solid hunting destination offering very good populations of buffalo—and excellent trophy quality—in both the Luangwa Valley areas in the east and the Kafue Plateau areas west of Lusaka. During the closure, there was definitely a lot of poaching, and squatters infiltrated some hunting blocks. At this writing, it's too early to analyze the full effects. Some blocks that were formerly very good are probably not quite so good now, but both the Kafue and Luangwa National Parks serve as vast reservoirs for buffalo, and I'm sure the overall numbers are still good. I've hunted Zambia four times and have taken some of my best bulls there, so I have a soft spot for this country.

At this writing, late 2004, Zimbabwe has some very serious political issues. A side effect to the squatters and the takeovers of private lands has been that the wonderful ranch hunting in the interior of the country is almost a thing of the past. The greatest loss, however, has been in plains game; because of the bovine disease problem, buffalo have been gone from most ranching country for decades. The periphery of the country—the Wankie corridor to the northwest, the entire Zambezi Valley to the north, and, thanks largely to private conservancies, even some of the southeastern lowveld—remains buffalo country. On Tribal Trust lands, forestry lands, and the valley areas administered by National Parks, Zimbabwe has done a wonderful job of managing her game. Tens of thousands of buffalo roam just as freely as they did when David Livingstone strode through. The thornbush is thick and the hunting rarely easy, but in spite of her current crisis, Zimbabwe still offers fine buffalo hunting.

Cape buffalo are surprisingly adaptable creatures. They must have water and grass, but otherwise they can occupy a wide variety of habitats. The swampy country of the Okavango Delta holds thousands of buffalo, and it isn't uncommon to catch a big herd like this moving from one island to another.

To the west, Botswana has tremendous numbers of buffalo in both the Okavango Delta and the Chobe region. There is pressure from cattle ranching and from citizen hunters; both the overall numbers and the available quota have shrunk considerably. The result is that Botswana can no longer compete with Zimbabwe and Mozambique in offering "short buffalo safaris." This is regrettable, but Botswana still holds plenty of buffalo and is a uniquely beautiful country, especially the Okavango.

Namibia is an extremely arid country, much of it occupied by either the Kalahari or the Namib Deserts. Thus, relatively little of Namibia is suitable buffalo habitat. There are a few areas in the far north, and, of course, the Caprivi Strip to the northeast is *all* buffalo habitat, though it was much depleted during the Angolan bush war (there is some buffalo hunting being done in the Caprivi, and it will get better over time, but opportunities will remain fairly limited for now). To Namibia's north, better-watered Angola is almost all buffalo country, at least historically. Like the D.R.C., Angola has "southern buffalo" in the south, transitioning to forest buffalo in the far north. The long civil war there was devastating to her wildlife, but some pockets remain, and adventuresome outfitters are already looking around. I expect there will be at least some hunting in Angola before this book is out of print, and buffalo will be on the menu.

South Africa's wonderful Kruger National Park holds tremendous numbers of buffalo, but these buffalo do nothing to increase the availability of buffalo to game ranchers (and, thus, to hunters). There is some buffalo hunting along the Kruger Park corridor, but although overall numbers are pretty good, South Africa's hunting opportunities for buffalo are very limited. As I said, this will increase over time, but unless things change dramatically, there are better places to hunt buffalo. This is simply because, in a supply and demand business, South African buffalo are, and probably will remain, comparatively very expensive.

So, all things considered, to my thinking, the primary countries for hunting Cape buffalo are Botswana, Mozambique, Tanzania, Zambia, and Zimbabwe. Please note that I listed them alphabetically. For trophy hunting, I have my favorites, and I'll cover those later. But don't hold me to these five. You can find good buffalo hunting wherever Cape buffalo roam. All you really need are good tracks and the will to follow them!

For the record, I have hunted Cape buffalo in Botswana, Kenya, Mozambique, Tanzania, Zimbabwe, and Zambia, several times in most of these countries. I have become a true junky on hunting the great black buffalo. Again, the variety in habitat types has been astounding: Thick *jess* in the Zambezi Valley; twelve thousand feet up on Mount Kenya; reedbeds and palm islands in the Okavango; *miombo* woodland in Zambia and Tanzania; mopane woodland in Zimbabwe. It's all wonderful, and the actual hunting doesn't vary a great deal.

You look until you find fresh tracks. If there are just a few, you look for bull tracks; if there are a number, you assume there must be bulls. You follow until you can look at the buffalo. Maybe the bull you want is there, maybe he isn't. If he is, you close for the shot. Maybe you get a shot, maybe you don't. Maybe you make a good shot, maybe you don't. If the latter, it can be a long day! But whatever happens, I can think of few things in life—and fewer hunts—that are more exciting from start to finish. And, as I alluded to earlier, while you're probably looking for a great bull (aren't we all, always?), the wonderful thing about Cape buffalo is that there doesn't have to be a great bull in the herd—or even a shot—for the hunting day to be one of those wonderful, golden memories. All you need to do is get close with the herd, and you'll have all the excitement you need!

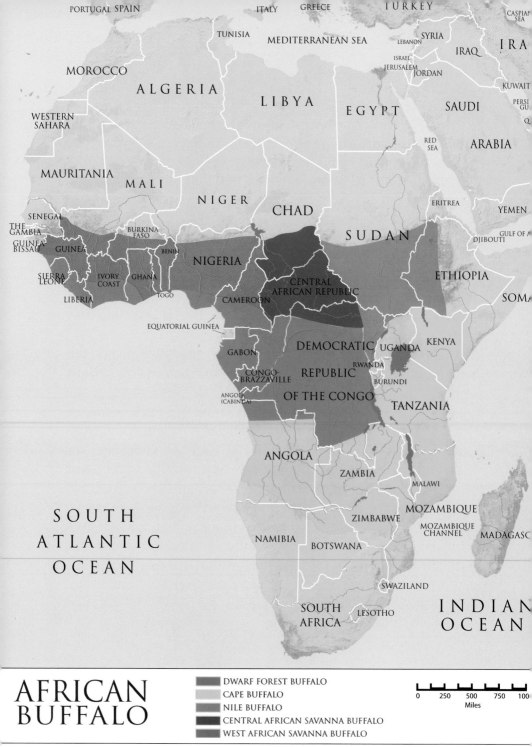

PORTUGAL SPAIN · ITALY · GREECE · TURKEY · CASPIAN SEA

TUNISIA · MEDITERRANEAN SEA · LEBANON · SYRIA · IRAQ · IRA

MOROCCO · ALGERIA · LIBYA · EGYPT · ISRAEL JERUSALEM · JORDAN · KUWAIT · PERSI GU · SAUDI · Q

WESTERN SAHARA · ARABIA · RED SEA

MAURITANIA · MALI · NIGER · CHAD · SUDAN · ERITREA · YEMEN · GULF OF · DJIBOUTI

SENEGAL · BURKINA FASO · NIGERIA · CENTRAL AFRICAN REPUBLIC · ETHIOPIA · SOM

THE GAMBIA · GUINEA BISSAU · GUINEA · BENIN

SIERRA LEONE · IVORY COAST · GHANA · TOGO · CAMEROON

LIBERIA · EQUATORIAL GUINEA

GABON · DEMOCRATIC · UGANDA · KENYA

CONGO-BRAZZAVILLE · RWANDA · REPUBLIC · BURUNDI

ANGOLA (CABINDA) · OF THE CONGO · TANZANIA

ANGOLA · ZAMBIA · MALAWI

MOZAMBIQUE

SOUTH ATLANTIC OCEAN · NAMIBIA · ZIMBABWE · MOZAMBIQUE CHANNEL · MADAGASC

BOTSWANA

SWAZILAND · INDIAN OCEAN

SOUTH AFRICA · LESOTHO

AFRICAN BUFFALO

DWARF FOREST BUFFALO
CAPE BUFFALO
NILE BUFFALO
CENTRAL AFRICAN SAVANNA BUFFALO
WEST AFRICAN SAVANNA BUFFALO

0   250   500   750   100
Miles

Africa's "other" buffalo lie generally to the north and northwest of the more widespread and plentiful Cape buffalo. The range for these other varieties is chiefly in the most remote parts of Africa, making the quest for any of these buffalo a most serious and specialized safari.

Africa's "Other" Buffalo
Chapter 3

As you move from east to west across the great bulge of Africa, the buffalo change gradually, but also very considerably. They get smaller in both body and horn, and instead of that classic boss, the horns start to diverge until they are actually separated by a strip of forehead of varying width. The southern buffalo is not only the most common, he is, by considerable margin, also the most impressive trophy. However, I think it's important—certainly for a volume like this—that we not forget Africa's "other" buffalo. Some of them, though lacking in headgear, are considerably harder to come by and prized much more by serious hunters. All of them are possessed of the same keen senses, ability to use cover, and wariness.

All of them are also equally dangerous, though perhaps for different reasons. Someone who should have known better once commented to me that "only the Cape buffalo counts as a member of the Big Five." That's ridiculous. Just because many hunters are simply unaware of Africa's other buffalo is no reason to discount them. The actual members of the Big Five—lion, leopard, buffalo, elephant, and rhino (black, white, or either, you choose!)—don't really care whether they're part of the club or not. The grouping was invented by humans, not the animals, and was meant to comprise Africa's dangerous game. I understand why the cheetah, almost never dangerous to man, has never been included (though, maybe we can discard the "almost"?). But, I honestly don't understand why the hippopotamus was never included! Regardless, if danger is a criterion, then it doesn't matter at all which buffalo you're talking about!

At least locally, the far western varieties actually have a much greater reputation for being aggressive than old *mbogo* himself. I have not hunted them enough to have any definitive knowledge, but for what it's worth, I do have an opinion. I tend to think that African buffalo are African buffalo. They are all much different from Asiatic water buffalo, and our American bison (and that animal's European counterpart), are even more miles apart. I believe the primary difference between the westernmost races and the southern buffalo is simply that buffalo in the west, especially in the forest zone, live in much thicker country. This means that the average encounter with humans is closer. Any animal that understands its ability to defend itself—and buffalo surely know this—is likely to be downright deadly when surprised at very close range.

Earlier this year, I was hunting along the Mayo Oldiri (*mayo* is the local word for river), in north-central Cameroon. The professional hunters and trackers there consider their buffalo very dangerous, which is smart, and give them plenty of respect, which is also smart. I wanted one of these buffalo, so we followed a number of herds. I did not find them any different from buffalo I have hunted a thousand miles and more to the east and south. However, in this very block, a buffalo killed a professional hunter just the season before. The story was that the hunter was minding his own business, just going from Point A to Point B. He walked onto a buffalo in very tall grass and was down before he had a chance. This could happen anywhere, and did, in Masailand, to poor Bob Fontana.

In general, the thicker the average cover, the more likely an incident. It is somewhat easier to stop a charge when you anticipate that one might be imminent, but even under the best circumstances, not all charges can be stopped, especially when launched from very close range. So I don't buy that the western races are more aggressive than any other African buffalo—but I absolutely agree that the thicker the cover, the more dangerous is *any* buffalo!

Scientists are not in agreement as to exactly how many races of buffalo there are. It is quite a difficult thing to determine, because the dividing lines are extremely unclear. There is also, especially in the western regions, tremendous variance in almost any given herd, not only with size and color, but even in horn configuration. For

Natural salt licks are scattered throughout the forest zone of Central Africa. They are natural gathering places for many varieties of wildlife. We surprised this herd of red buffalo at a lick in the southern C.A.R.

many years, the smallest race, the dwarf forest buffalo, was actually considered a separate species. Some authorities still hold this line, and there is some validity to their thoughts. But there are also broad, intergraded areas between the dwarf buffalo and the other races around him, so it becomes fairly clear that interbreeding is prevalent. I think Safari Club International has done a very good job of separating this mess into five races, with sensible, if not altogether scientific, boundaries. In addition to the Cape or southern buffalo, there are Nile buffalo, Central African savanna buffalo, West African savanna buffalo, and dwarf forest buffalo.

Nile Buffalo (*S. c. aequinoctialis*)

As the name properly suggests, this is the buffalo of the Nile drainage. At one time, he was undoubtedly found well up into Egypt, but today he is restricted to southern Sudan and adjacent Ethiopia, the northeastern D.R.C. along the Sudan border, and northwestern Uganda along the Albert Nile. To the southeast, he butts up against southern buffalo; to the southwest, dwarf forest buffalo; and to the west, Central African savanna buffalo. No one can say, and the buffalo certainly don't care, where one leaves off and the other properly begins. But when you're keeping records, you have to draw lines somewhere, and this makes as much sense as anything. On the Sudan/C.A.R. border, there won't be much difference in the buffalo from one side to the other, but Nile buffalo are definitely different from southern buffalo, and they begin a transformation that, on the western side of the continent, has become quite pronounced.

Nile buffalo are smaller, with weights suggested to run from eleven hundred to thirteen hundred pounds. More significant, they are no longer as predominantly black, with decidedly brown individuals common in the herds. This, of course, becomes more pronounced as you move westward. The horns still retain the general configuration of the Cape buffalo's—well hooked and with a pronounced boss—but they are considerably smaller, and rarely do their horns drop down alongside the jaw like the best southern buffalo do. As the SCI record book says, "Its smaller, flatter horns do not curve down to the level of the skull, so that when the skull is placed on the floor, the horns do not touch the floor."

When Sudan was being hunted, Nile buffalo were extremely common, and they were also plentiful in northern Uganda. With the more rare species, record book minimums are sometimes based on a fairly small sampling, but this is not the case with Nile buffalo. SCI's minimum, based on total length plus the widths of the bosses, is eighty. For southern buffalo, it is one hundred. This suggests that the Nile buffalo is, at least on average, 20 percent smaller, which falls right in line with its body weight. The world record, taken in the Mongalla region of Sudan, in 1977, scores 115⅜. So Nile buffalo aren't *that* small—that would be a darned good Cape buffalo, anywhere, anytime! But the comparison holds pretty well with the Cape buffalo world record, an amazing 141.

I have never hunted the Nile buffalo and, although I'd surely like to, there's a good chance I never will. There are certainly some left somewhere in the vastness of southern Sudan, but it's equally

Studying the horns of a Central African savanna buffalo at Trois Rivieres camp in the eastern C.A.R. As can clearly be seen, the horns of these buffalo are dramatically different from those of southern or Cape buffalo.

certain that the population has been greatly reduced by the now decades of bush war and famine. Uganda is closed, and although the D.R.C. is open, my guess is that the wildlife along the Sudan border has been virtually eradicated. The herd animals of the eastern C.A.R. were darn near wiped out in the early 1990s by meat poachers from Sudan, and I suspect the wildlife of northwestern Zaire and, for that matter, northern Uganda, probably suffered just as much. Currently, the only opportunity is Ethiopia, where there are scattered populations, but nowhere where buffalo remain plentiful. They are also much reduced in the Omo Valley of southern Ethiopia, and their current status in unknown in the Gambela region of western Ethiopia. This last area hasn't been hunted for years due to political turmoil, but some exploratory hunts are planned (with Nile lechwe as the primary goal). These forays might well turn up some Nile buffalo, but in Africa, political instability means hungry people, and that never bodes well for wildlife. Regrettably, neither the present nor the future is bright for this race of buffalo.

Central African Savanna Buffalo (*S. c. brachyceros*)

Until fairly recently, these buffalo, and all the buffalo to the west but north of the forest zone, were classed as "northwestern" buffalo. I tend to agree with the splitting off of these buffalo of the Central African Republic, southern Chad, and the northern edge of former Zaire (now the D.R.C.). They are smaller than the Nile buffalo, with weights estimated between eight hundred eighty and eleven hundred pounds. I am not altogether convinced that they are larger than the buffalo of northern Cameroon, as the books suggest, but taken in aggregate, their horns are not the same. Actually, they are a tremendous grab bag in terms of both body color and horn configuration. My feeling is that most (though not all) of the mature bulls of this subspecies are still black, or at least brown, but within any given herd, you will see animals ranging from tan through red through various shades of brown all the way to black. Some bulls have horns that look very much like Nile buffalo, with well-defined bosses, while others have the more

My old friend Bruno Scherrer with a very fine Central African savanna buffalo taken in the eastern C.A.R. This is a very wide-horned bull, with horns much more akin to what you might expect with a Nile buffalo—except that he is obviously red! (Photo by Rudy Lubin)

This is a Central African savanna buffalo, taken in the southern C.A.R., not far from Zaire. Color is a grab bag with these buffalo, as is horn configuration. This bull is obviously black, but his horns are much more like the dwarf forest buffalo than the southern buffalo.

divergent horns of the true dwarf forest buffalo. Note, of course, that the former are the bulls that will score the best according to the SCI system of measurement.

The most recent edition of SCI's record book lists more than one hundred of these buffalo, which is not a small sampling. The minimum score is sixty-five, which sounds a bit low. It probably isn't, since the world record score, a tie between Claude Garih and my old friend Jack Schwabland, is 96⅜ (these two trophies were taken, respectively, in 1966 and 1977). Note that this record-book high is well above the minimum for Nile buffalo, but also below the minimum for southern buffalo.

In 1992, we saw quite a lot of these buffalo along the Upper Chinko River. I made a mistake that year, one of my many in African hunting. I could have taken one, and probably a pretty good bull at that, but I was resolved to do no other shooting until I got my Derby eland. I didn't get one—or anything else! Two years later, I was back in the same area. This time I got a Derby eland, and we scratched around and got a pretty fair sampling of the other plains game. Regrettably, the Sudanese meat poachers had arrived in force. First, they'd taken the hippos—all of them—from the rivers, drying the meat and taking it back to Sudan in huge donkey caravans. Then, they'd turned to the buffalo, and these were mostly gone, as well. We saw a few tracks and ran into a few extremely wild survivors while tracking eland, but I never had a chance at one.

My first bongo hunt, in 1996, was in the southeastern C.A.R., not far from the Zaire border. There weren't a lot of buffalo around, but we did come upon a small herd one day after losing some bongo tracks. The bull I shot was black and relatively large in the body, but he had the divergent horn bases more common to the buffalo far to the west. I'm glad I took him, because it's quite possible that I'll never be in his part of Africa again. But, unlike the Nile buffalo, the Central African savanna buffalo remains quite common and quite huntable across much of the C.A.R. There is little wildlife left at all within a few dozen miles of the Sudan border, but the incursions have apparently been stopped, and this buffalo remains a normal part of the bag on most safaris in the "savanna" zone of C.A.R.

I put "savanna" in quotes because this is a bit of misnomer. There is true savanna and savanna woodland along the border with Chad, but most of what is called "savanna" in the C.A.R. is actually Terminalia forest, the term used to differentiate this relatively thick country from the *really thick*, true forests to the south. Remember, I shot my one and only Central African savanna buffalo while I was hunting bongo. For darned sure, that wasn't in any savanna! Farther north, where most of these buffalo are hunted today, the vegetation is generally about the same thickness as mopane forest in Zimbabwe. In other words, it's far from open, but it's a whole lot more open than the forest.

Of the more than one hundred Central African savanna buffalo currently listed in SCI, all but two were taken in the C.A.R. Of the two that weren't, one came from Chad, the other from northern D.R.C. This is not surprising. These buffalo almost certainly still exist in the D.R.C., but are probably smaller as they near the range of the dwarf forest buffalo. As for Chad, this country once had good numbers of buffalo, and they were huntable until the mid-1970s.

Even in the heart of the forest there are occasional clearings, and this is where the forest buffalo will feed. The problem is that they seem to be more nocturnal than savanna or southern buffalo, and hunting them in thick vegetation is very difficult.

Then, Chad closed for nearly twenty-five years. There was, and is, much poaching in her backcountry. Herd animals like buffalo are vulnerable. They go fast and, as we've noted, do not recover rapidly from disaster. In 2001, I hunted in extreme southern Chad, roadless, unmarked country along the Aoukele River. We were primarily looking for korrigum (Senegal hartebeest), and we found a few. Secretly, I was hoping to find buffalo, but we never saw a track. Since then, the outfitter, Alain Lefol, has found a few buffalo in remote pockets far from any villages, but this buffalo is clearly best hunted in the C.A.R.

West African Savanna Buffalo (S. c. planiceros)

This "race" of buffalo has only recently been split off by SCI, defined by them as occurring north of the forest zone, from Cameroon westward to the bulge of Africa. This encompasses a lot of country, but in recent years, the only hunting opportunities have been Cameroon, Burkina Faso, and Benin, so, at least from a hunter's standpoint, little is known about these buffalo except in these countries.

Although I'm more of a lumper than a splitter, I tend to agree with the division. By the time you get to Cameroon, the southern buffalo or Nile buffalo type of horns, with their closely knit, well-defined boss, are really gone. Obviously, some are much bigger than others (duh!), but the horns tend to be separated and to curve sharply upwards, rather than out.

Color remains a grab bag at least as far west as Burkina Faso. Some individuals are black, some are very red, and you can find almost anything of either sex or any age group. The size is supposed to be smaller—seven hundred to nine hundred pounds—and perhaps this is true as you progress farther westward. But if this is true in Cameroon, then the bull I shot was a real brute, smaller than a southern buffalo bull to be sure, but not by much! And one of his most interesting characteristics, aside from the rust coat with darker highlights on neck and shoulder, was that the inner surface of his ears were covered with long, soft *blond* hair.

Record-book listings continue to follow the curve, but it's fair to point out that there are only forty entries, so now we're down to a limited sampling. The minimum score is fifty-five, with the current world record, taken by Chuck Bazzy in Cameroon in 1984, scoring 81. Most of those forty entries came from Cameroon. This is not surprising since, of the three countries where this buffalo is hunted, Cameroon is far and away the most common destination. On the other hand, considering the few safaris taken to either place, both Benin and Burkina Faso are quite well represented. This suggests to me that all three countries—and probably other areas where no sport hunting is conducted—have pretty good populations of buffalo.

This was certainly the case in both the Mayo Oldiri and Mayo N'Duel blocks, where I hunted in 2003. We saw plenty of buffalo, running into herds almost every day. This was a unique hunt, at least in my experience. It was made so by a great outfitter who had super camps and wonderful areas; a really fine young Zimbabwean professional hunter named Guav Johnson; and

A good West African savanna buffalo from Cameroon. This is a big-bodied bull, bigger than these buffalo are supposed to be, but his horns are very typical. Some bulls are still black here, but this far west, red has become the predominant color.

Cameroon's weirdly strict game laws. Their game animals are divided into three classes: A, B, and C. Class A is the "good stuff" in the savanna, comprised of buffalo, roan, Derby eland, korrigum, lion, and elephant. I wasn't there for any of the last three, but choosing two from the first three was difficult. I love to hunt the spiral horns, and I consider Lord Derby's giant eland one of Africa's great trophies. On the other hand, I also love to hunt buffalo. I hadn't hunted this "newly created" type of buffalo, but I didn't care about that. What I did care about was that I really wanted a *red* buffalo. Ah, but then there was the roan. Western roan is the largest race of roan, and this area had some dandies.

At the outset, I decided not to decide, which must have confused the heck out of Guav. I told him we would hunt eland, roan, and buffalo until we had one of the three. Then we'd make another choice. The roan came first, and it was a wonderful bull. I still didn't decide; I told Guav we would now hunt eland and buffalo and let luck make the choice. We tracked some eland and twice, almost, but not quite, got a shot at a really magnificent bull. We also tracked buffalo, and I turned down several black bulls with really good horns. Remember, I wanted a red buffalo. This is kind of like turning down a huge black bear in favor of a smaller cinnamon bear, but that's what I wanted, and I was perfectly happy with following whatever tracks we came across, whether buffalo or eland.

The buffalo won. Or, better put, I suppose that individual bull lost. We picked up fresh tracks along a river, and as we followed, Guav pointed to a valley choked with tall grass, telling me that was where one of his colleagues had been killed the previous season. He also let slip that the same thing had almost happened to him in the same place: A buffalo had come out of nowhere in that thick grass, and he had been fortunate enough to stop it, literally, at his feet.

At the moment, that didn't bother me much, but it bothered me a whole bunch when I fluffed the shot and wounded my bull! During the previous week, we had followed buffalo for many hours, working several herds in really thick vegetation, trying to see the bulls. This one was a piece of cake. We followed for less than an hour, perfect wind in our faces, and we never saw the herd. We didn't need to, because a big-bodied, very mature, nicely horned, *red* bull was at the very rear. This area had burned recently, so it was even fairly open. We set up the shooting stick at about sixty yards, and when the bull turned broadside, I shot him too far forward, then shot right over him as he jinked up and over the next ridge. No excuses.

We had a chance a few seconds later when we topped the ridge, but this red bull didn't look hurt, so we let him top another ridge, then followed the blood trail right along his tracks. This sort of thing happens once in a while, but I don't like it. It's more embarrassing than it is frightening, but what I really don't like is putting my guide and his trackers at undue risk. I'd made the mess, and now we all had to go clean it up.

The trail was easy to follow and, of course, led straight through the burn. I have never seen a wounded buffalo stop in open country. Throughout their lives, heavy cover is their security blanket, and if they have enough vitality to reach it, they will. The burn stopped at the top of a gentle ridge, and in a little donga below, there was an evil patch of tall yellow grass. He had to be there, and it was my mess, so I followed the blood into that awful stuff. Nothing. Thank God!

We stopped to breathe a little on the far side, and I wiped the sweat from my palms. Just a few seconds had passed when Taiwee, our tall tracker, pointed up into the thick bush on the next ridge, maybe sixty yards above us. I stared and saw nothing, and then I saw a tail flick. The movement was gone immediately, but the buffalo was right there. I stared again, and then I saw a red body moving to the right. He hadn't seen us, so perhaps the smart money might have been to wait. I didn't wait, I wanted this over with. He was only partly visible through leaves, but I held where the chest must be and fired.

He was instantly gone from my sight, but now Guav could see him. "He's down," he said, and we all dashed up the hill to look at a really beautiful *red* buffalo.

Dwarf Forest Buffalo (S. c. nanus)

The other races differ from the southern buffalo by degree as you move westward, but the dwarf forest buffalo, also called "bush cow," is extremely different. Transition zones being as they are, some

This dwarf forest buffalo was shot with a .450 3¼-inch Nitro Express double. Too much for a small buffalo, true, but a good gun to have in case you meet an elephant in the rain forest. (Photo from Safari Press photo library)

A machan overlooking a bai *or swampy clearing deep in the forest. From such a lookout one might see bongo, forest sitatunga, or forest buffalo. Or, as happened with me, one might spend several days and see nothing, despite plenty of tracks.*

of the buffalo that pass for dwarf buffalo probably are not, but the real dwarf buffalo is truly a runt. He weighs little more than six hundred pounds, not a whole lot heavier than a really big bongo. The small horns curve upward, and rarely do the animals have any semblance of boss whatsoever. Color varies from light tan to dark brown, but should not be pure black. A fringe of hair in the ears, like that bull I shot in Cameroon, is normal.

Uniquely, this buffalo differs genetically from the other races. All the rest have fifty-two chromosomes, while the dwarf buffalo has fifty-four. His extremely different size and appearance caused earlier naturalists to consider him a separate species, and the chromosomal facts support that conclusion. But he clearly interbreeds freely with other buffalo all along the fringes of his range (which borders all other buffalo), so I tend to believe the hypothesis that there is just one African buffalo despite distinct racial characteristics.

The dwarf buffalo actually inhabits a very large range, virtually the entire forest zone of Central and West Africa, from northern Angola up along the coast to Congo-Brazzaville and Gabon; on through the entire coastal forest zone of West Africa all the way to Liberia; and eastward through most of the D.R.C., southern Cameroon, and the southwestern corner of C.A.R. Wherever he occurs, he is the very devil to hunt because of the dense forest he inhabits!

The SCI record book has forty-five entries, which I consider a pretty good number, considering the difficulty in hunting this animal. The minimum score is forty, and the world record, taken on the Sangha River in the southwestern C.A.R., scores 68⅝. Again, these figures track well with the reduction in body size, and all the record listings hang together nicely in support of the five different classifications.

Current hunting opportunity for the dwarf forest buffalo is probably best in southern Cameroon, although the D.R.C. will probably be even better when, and if, its new hunting program gets going. However, there is no clear-cut winner among those forty-five listings. Cameroon is well represented, but so are southwestern C.A.R., Gabon, Liberia, Congo-Brazzaville, and the D.R.C. There are also a couple of old entries from northern Angola, one taken by the great Italian hunter Dr. Carlo Caldesi in 1966. A second entry appears courtesy of one of my great heroes, George Parker, in 1952, coincidentally the year I was born! (For the record, on that safari, Parker also became one of very, very few sportsmen to take a giant sable.)

Many of these areas are not currently open, but hunting comes and goes as the political pendulum swings back and forth in this difficult region. With such a broad range, there should be plenty of opportunity to hunt this buffalo. I hope there is, because at this writing, a dwarf forest buffalo is one of the trophies I want most. I took my bongo halfway through a hunt on the Sangha River, in that little corner of the southwestern C.A.R., with Jean-Christophe Lefol, Alain Lefol's nephew. We spent the rest of the safari trying to get a buffalo, so I know a very little bit about them.

While they definitely live in the forest, dwarf forest buffalo do come out into the rare clearings to feed, and you also often find them in open swampy areas. While all the other races seem to be found in herds of almost any size, depending on population, it seems that dwarf buffalo are more likely found in much smaller family groups. My interest in them is such that I tend to keep my ears open, and I have never heard of a big herd. I also tend to think they are more nocturnal than most other buffalo—but that could be time and place. For darn sure they were nocturnal—and invisible!—where I hunted them. I just hope there will be another time and place.

Following the Tracks
Chapter 4

Y ou've been sitting in the back of the truck since dawn, and now the morning is heating up fast. It's been slow; early on, that nice kudu bull flashed across the road, but it's been a while since you've even seen an impala. Your attention span ran out long ago, and as much as you try to fight it, your thoughts aren't in Africa, but back in the office you came here to escape. The Land Cruiser stops and the trackers jump down, but this has happened several times, and you're no longer paying attention.

Now your professional hunter gets out, and he and the trackers huddle in the middle of the road. The trackers walk slowly into the brush, zigzagging this way and that, attention focused downward. Your PH walks back toward you, and suddenly you're back in Africa. "I think we'll follow these," he says. "It's a big herd, and they crossed sometime after sunrise."

Buffalo hunting really starts when fresh tracks are found. Chances are you will see other game while you're looking, and depending on your goals and available licenses or quota, you might pick up a great trophy or two along the way. You might even see a herd of buffalo, but although you think that's what you're looking for, you really aren't. An impala for the pot is one thing, but the last thing in the world you want to do with buffalo is shoot one from the truck.

If you see buffalo, you will probably stop the vehicle immediately and let them fade into the cover before beginning the hunt. In really open country, you might well see buffalo at a distance, glass them, and begin the stalk with no tracking at all. I have done this several times in Tanzania, and a couple of times on the flood plains around Botswana's Okavango. But in most buffalo country, the cover is too thick and the vistas are limited. If you see buffalo, they will almost certainly spook, so you will wait a few minutes and begin tracking from the last place you saw them. But you'd have been better off finding their fresh tracks and following a completely unalarmed herd.

So, again, what you're really looking for are tracks that are fresh enough to follow. Depending on buffalo density, the search might be very simple. Or it might be very long and very boring. In really great buffalo areas like much of the Zambezi Valley and the Selous Reserve, I have, literally, been into buffalo every single day of a safari. But even in these great areas, the prevailing conditions, particularly the availability of water and good grazing, have a tremendous impact on buffalo concentrations. Even the very best areas rarely hold the same numbers of buffalo throughout the season, and, today, most hunting areas have boundaries that cannot be crossed, whether a neighboring hunting area or a park boundary.

Once in a while it's possible to glass buffalo moving in the early morning or late afternoon. This was a great vantage point in the hills above the Zambezi Valley, and I've done the same thing in Masailand. Most of the time, though, you're just looking for tracks.

This track looks pretty good, but it was a windy morning, and there was an awful lot of grass in the track. The trackers will study this and can determine whether the debris was stepped on or was blown in.

Rainfall can be fickle, and if there are better water and grass on the other side of that boundary, well, you're in for tough sledding. This has happened to me in some really great buffalo areas. In 1977, I hunted along the eastern edge of Kenya's Tsavo National Park, normally a fine buffalo area. Short rains had hit the park, but had not hit our hunting block. I was there two weeks, and not a single buffalo ever crossed out of the park. It was much the same in Zambia's Luangwa Valley, in 1983. I was hunting the area between Luangwa North and South, normally a great area for buffalo—but not at the time I was there. Some of the other hunters in our party took buffalo, but neither my partner nor I ever had tracks to follow.

Thankfully, this is rare. It's also rare, even in really good country, to get into buffalo every day. I've had this kind of luck only two or three times, even though I've spent many safaris in really good buffalo country. To be truthful, looking for tracks can be downright boring, if that word can ever be used to describe Africa. Usually you will see other game along the way, but often not a great deal. Much of the best buffalo country (like Zimbabwe's mopane woodland and *jess* and the *miombo* forest of Zambia and southern Tanzania), simply doesn't hold concentrations of plains game. Also, visibility is generally restricted. You'll see the odd flash of this and that, but if you're hunting buffalo, you're really concentrating on finding tracks.

This single-minded focus is becoming much more prevalent in today's Africa. As game quotas shrink and prices increase, safaris are becoming ever more specialized. It wasn't long ago that a genuine, specialized buffalo safari was almost unheard of. Clear through the 1980s, licenses in many countries were more or less "open": If you saw it, liked it, and could afford the trophy fee, you could shoot it. So you wanted a buffalo, fine. You looked for tracks, but you were also hunting for whatever else might have been of interest along the way. If you didn't find buffalo tracks today, no problem. Chances are you found something else you desired, and in the morning you can look for buffalo tracks again.

My first safari with Geoff and Russ Broom, in Zambia, in 1984, was not only a classic of this sort of smorgasbord safari, but the first part of it was also the most incredible run of luck I've ever had. Geoff turned me over to his son, Russ, just out of college in the 'States, for the first week or so. I wanted a good buffalo (of course), but I also wanted a good sable. Sable didn't occur in their Luangwa concessions, so Russ took me to the Namwala and Mumbwa blocks adjoining the Kafue National Park. In those days, Zambia didn't require the purchase of licenses in advance; it was a pure trophy fee system. So we put up some lion and leopard baits just in case, and every morning we left camp looking for buffalo.

We cut some tracks headed back into the park and even saw a few buffalo standing on the wrong side of the boundary, but we had only a couple days left in the area before we actually got into buffalo. I took a massive old bull that still ranks as one of my best, but at that time, I'm not sure it mattered a great deal. While looking for buffalo tracks, I took my best sable, my best lion, a huge Livingstone's eland, an incredible Lichtenstein's hartebeest, and I don't know what all else.

A good, clean print, photographed in late morning and almost certainly made well after dawn the same day. We could follow these tracks.

This sort of thing is very rare today and only available on lengthy and very expensive safaris in just a couple of countries, primarily Tanzania and Zambia. Quotas are such that, on shorter safaris, regardless of the game you might see (and it *is* wonderful to see it), there may not be much besides buffalo available on quota. In July 2004, I hunted in the Sapi area of the Zambezi Valley with Andrew Dawson and Paul Smith's Chifuti Safaris. I was there to make a film on buffalo hunting, and I had two buffalo on quota. After all these years, there really wasn't much else that I wanted, but I was truly shocked at how little flexibility there was. In that season, Andrew and Paul had something like thirty buffalo bulls and ten cows on quota. At the same time, they had four waterbuck, four warthog, maybe five kudu, four zebra, and so forth. Obviously the key plains game needed to be allocated to longer safaris that included lion or leopard, and the only game quotas that were larger than buffalo were impala and baboon.

This was perfectly fine by me. While hunting buffalo I took a wonderful Sharpe grysbok and, through incredible blind luck, a huge hyena. Andrew's quota isn't large for either animal, but nobody books a safari for grysbok or hyena, and the chances of getting either are quite slim. So I was very lucky to see them, the animals were available, and it was wonderful. We saw a lot of other game—kudu, waterbuck, warthog, and even a few nyala. We also saw a really great lion, one of the best I've seen in many years. I'm accustomed to not being able to take a lion as a "target of opportunity," and it's been many years since such a thing was a likely scenario. But, it was an odd feeling to know that should we chance upon a sixty-inch greater kudu, all I would be permitted to do would be to enjoy looking at him.

This is the way things are going in Africa. Increasingly, a "buffalo safari" of ten days or so in good buffalo country will have relatively little other game available. Probably impala, maybe warthog, maybe the oddball game (like my grysbok and hyena), that isn't "spoken for." This isn't the way it used to be, isn't like you read about in books of a time before this one, but it is the reality of modern Africa. Since I can't turn back the clock, I think that's just fine, but it means the mindset needs to change. A good

Once you start a buffalo track, you have no idea where it might lead or how long it might be before you make contact. As the day wears on and the tracks keep going, it is difficult to keep your attention focused on the job, but you must, because somewhere, anywhere, there are buffalo in the bush ahead of you.

Zimbabwe professional hunter Rory Muil checks out a pool left behind as the waters recede from one of the Zambezi's many tributaries. Buffalo must water almost every day, so as the dry season progresses and water sources become more limited, the more concentrated they will be.

buffalo is a great trophy, and getting him is a great hunt. That's all right by me, and it should be for anyone who wants the same. In the same amount of time it takes to hunt buffalo properly, you can take a dozen species of plains game in Namibia or South Africa—but they aren't buffalo country. So hunt your plains game first to get it out of your system, and then get serious about buffalo. Expect some boredom while you're looking for tracks, though it will undoubtedly be mixed with excitement when you see great trophies that aren't available to you. And wait for the time that will come, sooner or later, when your PH will say, "I think we should follow this herd."

On the Tracks

You dismount from the hunt car, drink some water, load your rifle, and make sure you have everything you need. And then you step forth on one of the great adventures remaining in our modern world. If your hands don't have a slight tremor and if your palms don't sweat just a little bit, then I feel sorry for you. Either you are sadly lacking in imagination or you are so cool that you really should consider golf or tennis instead of hunting. *This is the real thing.* You are headed toward a face-to-face encounter with one of the world's most dangerous animals.

Most of the time, this apprehension is extremely premature. Your professional hunter and his trackers believe the tracks are fresh enough to follow. This means that, in their experience—based not only on exactly how recently the buffalo passed, but also on their knowledge of buffalo movement in the area—you have a good chance of catching up. Fine, but only the buffalo determine what happens next: That's the wonderful thing about taking buffalo tracks, you have no idea what might happen once you start to follow them—but chances are you've got some walking ahead of you before you need to turn on the adrenaline!

Some professional hunters are lazy, others are more aggressive. Trackers are the same. But nobody wants to follow tracks unless there's a good chance of catching up. So I take it as

Zimbabwe professional hunter Andrew Dawson and I take a break at a hidden spring in some hills above the Zambezi Valley. Small springs like this will hold buffalo long after the water holes in the bush are dry, so such locations are prized information.

Depending on the circumstances and if fresh tracks aren't found, you might return to camp at midday, or you might stay out for the whole day. On this day, we got a treat for lunch: Traditional sudza *with meat stew, cooked over a mopane fire.*

an article of faith that if the PH and the trackers are in agreement, it's likely you can close with the buffalo. This is not certain. Tracking is an art, rather than a science, and sometimes you walk quite a ways only to discover the tracks weren't quite as fresh as advertised. But even if they're fresher than you thought they were, the buffalo were on the move when they were made, and only they will determine when they will stop. So you're going to walk on the tracks, and you have no idea how far they will take you or what you will find at their end.

The walking is generally not difficult. If it's a big herd, the spoor is easy to follow and the trackers will walk at a normal pace. If it's just a couple of bulls, the tracking will be slow and painstaking, with many stops while the experts cast ahead and to the sides for spoor. At first the going is easy, but be careful, you don't know how long this will go on.

The proper shoes for African hunting must be comfortable, but must also be very quiet. Good choices include Russell, Courtenay, and Oakley, although many hunters do just fine with high-topped tennis shoes. For clothing, I like to wear shorts because they are cool and quiet. Just remember, if you wear shorts, you are going to get scratched by thorns. I don't mind, but that's up to you. Twenty years ago, I tended to wear broad-brimmed hats. After all, that's what African hunters wear, right? Today, I am much more likely to wear a baseball cap because I've since learned that "safari hats" catch in brush and blow off in the vehicle. I also wear and carry sunscreen.

The most important tip I can offer is to drink lots of water. Often. Excitement only delays dehydration. Most African hunting is done during the winter months, when the weather is deceptively balmy. You may not feel it, but you're losing moisture by the minute, and it must be replaced. Drink a liter of water before you start on the tracks, and take a drink every time you stop. I usually carry a bit of water myself, but any PH worthy of the title will ensure that his crew is carrying enough for even the longest tracking job.

How long might that be? Again, only the buffalo know. I have tremendous faith in African trackers. They aren't into wild goose

This old dugga boy, taken in Zambia's Kafue region, was at the end of the shortest tracking job I've ever been on. He was a lone bull, usually a chancy thing to follow, but we weren't looking for a trophy buffalo that day, and we caught him in about an hour.

chases. If they believe tracks are worth following, then I accept that as Gospel. This does not mean you will get a shot. Once in a while, buffalo will just keep on walking. Sometimes the wind does a one-eighty, and that's the end of the game. More often you catch the herd toward midday, when the wind is most unstable, and after hours of perfect tracking, your scent betrays you. Even if things work perfectly, there is no guarantee the bull you want is with this herd. Depending on how picky you are, there's a strong likelihood that he is not. But in order to find out, you must see the herd.

In my experience, if the trackers want to follow a herd, the chances of seeing them are very good. How many hours of tracking this might require is up for grabs. The shortest buffalo hunt I ever made was in Zambia, in 1995. I was in the Mulobezi block with Russ Broom, and our sole purpose there was to take a buffalo. In fact, we wanted to do this as quickly as possible so we could proceed to the Bangweulu for our main objective there, a good sitatunga.

It was July, early in the season, as things go in the Kafue area. There was still plenty of water in the national park, so the only buffalo in the hunting area were a few *dugga* boys hanging around water holes. We checked several of these for tracks and, in the process, we enjoyed one of the most incredible processions of African wildlife I have ever seen. Before we saw the first buffalo track, we saw lion, eland, sable, zebra, waterbuck, hartebeest, impala, reedbuck, warthog, giraffe, and more.

And then we found the morning tracks of a big-bodied buffalo bull at a water hole nestled in an open *dambo*. We followed him, and in less than an hour, Russ stopped and put up his binoculars. I have no idea what he thought he saw, but this is not the norm. More often the trackers, walking ahead with gifted eyesight, see the game first. Not this time. I tried, but all I could see was a bit of black—I guess that was what I was supposed to see! All on full alert now, we crept a bit closer, and when the bull got up, I shot him, only an hour's walk from the vehicle.

In my experience, this is unusual. I can recall a few times when we've caught up more quickly with buffalo we've actually seen, but this stands as the shortest "pure" tracking job I've ever been part

Trackers Lummock, Sheki, and Mukasa pose proudly with a nice Zambezi Valley bull. Good trackers truly make the hunt. Their skill must not be underestimated, nor their courage: They go in first, unarmed, placing their lives in the hands of the PH.

of. The longest is hard to define, because I've spent many hours on buffalo tracks for negative results: Bad wind, no good bulls, animals crossing park boundaries, and so forth. There have been so many unsuccessful tracking jobs that it's the successful ones that stick in my mind. I think the longest occurred in 1988, in the Selous Reserve.

We were at the tail end of the safari, the last hunting day, and I wanted to take one final buffalo. It was late morning and hot when we found the tracks of perhaps a dozen bulls. The herd had traveled straight down the road for a half-mile or so, giving us a really good look at the spoor. It was clearly quite fresh, with the dung still warm. After a while, the tracks veered off the road into relatively open forest on the right. Perfect. Professional hunter Paddy Curtis pulled the truck into a patch of shade, and we quickly grabbed our rifles and started out.

At this time of day, with tracks this fresh, we expected to make contact very quickly. Not quite! The tracks ran dead straight for miles, and before too long, it was clear the buffalo were outdistancing us. I really can't explain this. There was one point where the wind was a bit dicey, so it's possible that they got a bit of our scent and just kept going, but we never encountered running tracks. Perhaps they were just on some kind of a bovine mission. It wasn't hard tracking, so we kept going, as well. Had we found running tracks, we probably would have waved off, and had this been any other hunting day, we probably would have quit eventually and put the time to better use. But this was the last day and we had nothing else going, so we kept after them. Surely they must stop eventually?

I think it was pushing four o'clock before we finally caught up, after some six hours of steady walking on the tracks. This is not unusual when tracking giant eland, and it is fairly routine with elephant, but that's a long tracking job to make first contact with buffalo, especially when the tracks are fresh at the start. When we found them, they were bedded peacefully at the top of a little knoll, spread out in a circle and completely at rest. By this time, judging from the spoor, they had probably been there a couple of hours.

Paddy and I crawled in fairly close and looked them over. Surprisingly, for a bachelor herd this size, there were no really old bulls, nor were any of them particularly large. Maybe that's a partial answer; lazy old bulls wouldn't normally walk that far, but these youngsters certainly did! On any other day, we might have turned back for the truck. But we were now just a few hours from dark on the last day of the hunt.

So we looked them over very carefully, and there was only one nice-looking bull with hard bosses, all the rest still soft. Of course, that one bull was on the wrong side of the group, so we crawled around to get a better angle. We were almost there when they began to stand up. It was time for them to begin feeding again, but I'm not sure whether this was their goal or whether one of them saw some movement. Whichever, when our bull stood, I shot him in the lungs with my old Andrews .470. Instantly, there were buffalo running everywhere, and there was no opportunity for a second shot. But then, there was no need for one. He was down, just sixty yards away and seemingly dead, but I paid the insurance anyway, and we set him up for some quick photos.

With fresh bull tracks so late in the morning, we had made a huge mistake, leaving the truck with no water at all. It had been hot, and now I was desperately thirsty. I have never again started off on a buffalo track without making sure we had at least some water! The November short rains had started, and there were a few reasonably clear pools around. Paddy drank from one of these, but I decided I wasn't quite that thirsty yet! I stayed with the buffalo and enjoyed the rest of my last afternoon, while Paddy and the crew hot-footed it for the distant Toyota. It was starting to get dark when I heard the vehicle crashing through the brush. I was mighty glad to see them, but far happier to get my hands on a water bottle!

How Fresh Are the Tracks?

Tracking is very much an art, rather than a science. Finding and recognizing buffalo tracks is not difficult, nor is it difficult to determine bull tracks from the significantly smaller cow tracks. The hard part is aging the tracks, but there are clues. Leaves and debris will have fallen into really old tracks, and this is also very easy to determine. The really difficult task is separating last night's tracks from this morning's tracks. The edges will sometimes provide the answer. On really fresh tracks, the edges are clean and sharp, but as time goes on, even slight breezes will cause the edges to crumble and fade. Of course, this depends a lot on the soil and also on the wind. Often it's necessary to follow the tracks long enough to find some dung in order to be sure. Buffalo defecate frequently while moving and feeding. With a herd, it usually doesn't take long to find some dung, but the fewer the buffalo, the longer you might have to follow.

Browsing animals like eland and kudu offer other clues (such as freshly bitten leaves and twigs), but buffalo dung provides the acid test for how fresh the spoor really is. And like the tracks, aging dung, too, is an art. In midday sun, droppings dry quickly, forming a hard crust and turning black. But in shade and morning cool, they appear very fresh for quite a long time. As you're tracking, you will see the trackers take a foot and scuff over a crusted buffalo patty, seeing how thick the crust is. When they think they're getting close, they will put a finger into the dung, checking the temperature. When it's blood warm, they know the buffalo are close. By now the ash bags are out, and they are constantly checking the wind.

Exactly how fresh tracks should be before they're worth following is yet another piece of the trackers' craft. Buffalo will normally be moving and feeding from about four o'clock in the afternoon until dark. They will alternate between feeding and resting throughout the night, and in the early morning hours, they should be on the move again. So, during the morning hunt, tracks that appear reasonably fresh might be anything from a few minutes to eighteen hours old. Obviously, you want to follow morning tracks that are just a couple hours old. But this depends on buffalo density and also the local movement patterns.

Most buffalo will lie down between midmorning and late afternoon, so in the morning, you have all day to catch up. If you're

In burned areas, tracks are extremely distinct, and it's also very easy to see how fresh they are because ash, being light, will blow in and out with the slightest breeze.

having trouble finding buffalo tracks at all, you might well follow spoor from early the previous evening. Depending on the network of hunting tracks in the area, you may drive this way and that, seeing if the herd has crossed another road and thus offered a shortcut. With the day ahead of you, chances are pretty darned good that you can close on any buffalo that clearly passed during hours of darkness the night before.

The afternoon is entirely different. Now you have just a couple of hours before dark, so afternoon tracks must be very fresh. Remember, too, that in the late afternoon, buffalo will be moving and feeding. Their progress will be very slow, so if afternoon tracks are smoking fresh, you have a good opportunity to close. It's definitely worth a try, because it's much easier to work a moving herd, and also because buffalo are usually calm and will be moving along very slowly in the evening. Sometimes you won't catch up, and even if you do, it might get dark before you either get a shot or see all the bulls. But that's also just fine, because you have a known starting point to resume the hunt at first light.

Trackers and Professional Hunters

The powers of observation of a good African tracker are simply amazing and a pure joy to watch. I cannot see what they can see, and I cannot do what they can do. These guys grew up in the bush, and their ability to see game, as well as simply track, often seems downright uncanny. Some experienced professional hunters cannot track at all, but a few, and only the best, are almost as good as the trackers. This is especially true of most of the Zimbabwe hunters who, like the previous generation of East African hunters, grew up in the bush hunting elephant and buffalo. Today, I believe the Zimbabwe professional hunters, as a group, are the finest in Africa. But all professional hunters who hunt dangerous game rely heavily on their trackers.

It's very much a team effort based on an incredible level of mutual trust. The trackers must concentrate on the spoor, studying the ground as they walk, but even so, with their amazing bush eyes and walking slightly ahead, they will often see the game

Tracker Mukasa and PH Andrew Dawson confer on buffalo movement. Good PHs and their trackers have a very special relationship based on mutual trust borne from shared danger—and make no mistake, good trackers are at least as important as a competent professional.

first. This, however, is really the professional hunter's job. He must rely on the trackers to hold the track while he keeps his full attention ahead and to the sides. In return, the trackers absolutely rely on him to ensure their safety. You and I, the hunting clients, are really not part of this mix. We are untested and untried, we come and go, and, all too often, we screw up. Then the professional hunter and his trackers must wade into the thick vegetation and clean up our messes. Most good professional hunters and their equally good trackers develop a very close relationship that lasts for many years, more of a friendship based on mutual trust and respect than an employee/employer relationship, and this bond has probably been tested in many tight spots over the years.

There is some African hunting literature out there that suggests the trackers will run away at the first hint of danger. This angers me tremendously. The raw courage of the African trackers has always and consistently amazed me. They go in first, unarmed, and the level of faith they place in their professional hunter and his rifle is also amazing. They will follow the spoor wherever it leads, wounded or unwounded, no matter how thick the country. Chances are they will see the game first, and then they will assist the professional hunter in maneuvering you and me, the clumsy clients, for a shot. Now, if there is a charge, it is absolutely true that they will scatter. Fast. This is also their job—to get out of the way so the rifles can be employed. They take the greatest risk, and all too many of them bear scars to prove it. For me, one of the great joys in African hunting is watching these true professionals at work. And some of the very best tracking is done on the spoor of buffalo.

Getting Close

Chapter 5

I f you're lucky, you've walked on the tracks for an hour or two. If, however, you're not lucky, you've been on them most of the day. The walking isn't difficult and certainly isn't fast, but there's been plenty of it. It's hot now, and you're tired. At the beginning, you were on full alert and ready, but now your attention span is short. You're daydreaming as you walk, and the rifle, heavy now, hangs from its sling or balances carelessly on your shoulder.

The trackers are going carefully now, checking dung frequently and shaking their ash bags. They believe the buffalo are close. But you've heard that before, maybe several times during that day, and it's hard to shake off the midday stupor. Then the lead tracker freezes in midstride and extends an open palm backward. You stop, and almost magically the rifle appears in your hands at high port. Suddenly, you aren't tired any more. Not at all.

This is the point Jacques Lemaux, a wonderful French PH who I hunted with in the Central African Republic, called "making contact." Someone has seen *something*. Your professional hunter steps forward, slowly, and cranes his head toward the tracker so his eyes are on the same plane and seeing the same things. The tracker points into the dense bush ahead. He might point with an extended finger or he might use a short stick. My first trackers, Musili and Muindi, were Wakamba, a great hunting tribe of East Africa. They believed pointing with an extended finger would instantly alert the game, so they pointed with a curled index finger, only the first knuckle extended and the fingertip pointing back.

You might think an animal the size of a buffalo would be easy to see. This is true if you catch them grazing in an open green *dambo*.

It is not true if you catch them in their resting cover, places thick and nasty and dappled with black, midday shadows. You are looking for black animals or, more likely, pieces of black animals among that black shadow. Sometimes the visibility is a hundred yards or more, but more often it's half that—or half that again.

Don't feel bad if you have trouble seeing what your mentors see. It's difficult, and I have no idea how much experience is required before it becomes easy. I have made contact with buffalo hundreds of times now, and when they're in thick vegetation it's still difficult for me to make them out. Your hunting team won't get it right all the time. When they know you're getting close, they will slow down and they will look ahead more. They will stop and look hard at suspicious black patches, sometimes motioning the PH to join them so that he can look with his binocular. There might be several of these dry runs, but sooner or later the PH will slowly nod, and then he will motion you forward.

If the animals are still moving, it won't be difficult to pick them out, even in the thickest bush. If they're stationary it will be harder,

When game is sighted Jacques Lemaux, my old friend and C.A.R. professional hunter, calls it "making contact." PH Cliff Walker and I have just made contact with buffalo, and now it's time to get close.

and if they're lying down it will be really tough. The tendency is to get frustrated. "Hell, I can't see him!" you want to shout. It's easier to say than to do, but keep calm and *look*. My suspicion is good Eastern whitetail hunters are better at this than I am, a Western hunter more accustomed to glassing big country with a binocular. You may want to use your binocular—especially if your PH is using his. Look for horizontal lines in vertical brush. Look for the curve of a horn, the twitch of an ear, the swish of a tail. Look for coal black, blacker than the shadows. Look for the glint of sun on polished horn or wet muzzle. Take your time and don't get shook. The buffalo are right there. You have time. Ah, there it is. And then another. It all comes clear. And now begins the really fun part of buffalo hunting, working the herd, sorting the bulls. Getting *close*.

Watching the Wind

At this stage, the wind is the most important thing of all. Now, if the wind wasn't good to begin with, you wouldn't have gotten this close. But one puff of human scent now, and the herd will be in motion, kicking up dust as they gallop away. Then the tracking job starts all over. Except it will be more difficult the next time you make contact because the herd has been alerted and will be on edge.

Typically, undisturbed buffalo will more or less feed into the wind, more concerned about what lies ahead than behind. But now that you're near them, playing the wind is critical. It is also more complicated. Whether the country is very open or very thick, you will probably have to move around a bit to see what kind of bulls the herd holds. You have to keep the wind in your favor at all times, so there will be some directions you can go and some avenues that are blocked. The trackers think about wind all the time, and now they are monitoring it, usually with ash bags, small, porous pokes filled with fine white ash that puffs out like fine smoke when the bag is shaken. This is the critical part.

The complicated part is that if your tracking job has taken you into the midday hours, it is now very warm and, normally, the African winds have become unstable. There will be unpredictable swirls and eddies, and any of them can give you away. While tracking, if the winds become unsteady or start to shift, the trackers will often take you away from the track, only circling around to cut the track again when the prevailing breeze has reasserted itself.

Once contact is made, the trackers will do the same thing again. If the herd is still moving, this is relatively simple, but if the herd is lying down, it may be impossible to close in. African winds aren't any more predictable than anywhere else, but most of the time you can expect a reasonably steady breeze until late morning. After that you can expect swirling breezes and stray gusts until late afternoon, when the wind usually becomes consistent once more.

Even with the best trackers and best of intentions, sometimes you're going to spook the herd. Usually it's one of those stray puffs of ill wind, but a sharp-eyed cow might spot you or an unseen buffalo may pop up out of nowhere and give the whole show away. This, too, is frustrating. Just how much depends on how long the tracking job, how many days you've been looking for buffalo, and whether you've gotten a glimpse of a really big bull. When they go, it's spectacular, a thunder of moving bodies raising a great

Trackers Mukasa and Lummock filling their ash bags at the fireplace; they prefer fine, white, mopane ash. When shaken, these porous bags give a puff of white smoke, an ideal tool for making certain of wind direction.

Now is the time to move in slowly and carefully, single file, probably just you and your professional hunter. Your palms begin to sweat and your heart is racing. This is the best part of any buffalo hunt.

plume of dust, with cattle smell filling your nostrils and cattle sounds filling your ears. This *is* going to happen, and it may happen many times. Enjoy the show, and get ready to do some more walking!

Sorting the Bulls

Once you've made contact, it probably won't be difficult to shoot a buffalo—if all you want to do is shoot a buffalo. In the old days (actually not so long ago), when trophy fees were a fraction of what they are today, and when multiple buffalo on license was common, the goal was often to simply make contact, get close enough for a good shot, and take any bull, perhaps for a lion bait, perhaps for rations. Things are different today, and, on the whole, I like it better. I sure don't like the higher trophy fees, but I do like the elevated trophy status of good buffalo, and I don't mind that there's usually just one buffalo on license or available on quota. It makes you more careful, it makes you hunt harder, and it requires that you sort the bulls, looking for the best one you can find.

In any group, small or large, the mission is to see all the bulls. But this isn't particularly easy, even with a moving herd in relatively open country. There are always other animals in the way, and if you can see the buffalo, then they can see you. So you must use available cover, which limits your approach options. In thick cover—hell, even with relatively small groups, it's almost impossible to see all the bulls. But this is what you are trying to do, and that's both the hard part and the fun part.

Working a group of buffalo, trying to see all the bulls (at least until you see the one you want), is a lot like having a time bomb in your hands with no knowledge of when it might go off. Sooner or later, they're going to explode. That is almost a given. In big herds, you will probably never see all the bulls before this happens. In smaller groups, you may have a chance, especially if you are able to get onto them two or three times. With elephant hunting, I figure you've won if you see the ivory of the bull you're following, even if it's no good and even if it took you twenty hard miles to see the tusks. With buffalo, I feel really good walking back to the truck, with no

Sometimes you simply have to wait them out. This was another last-day bull, taken in Tanzania. The herd was just starting to lie down when we made contact. We waited nearly five hours before they started to get up, and then we finally got a shot.

shots fired, if I know I looked at all of them and the one I wanted just wasn't there. But this feeling is rare!

One day this past July, just before sundown, we took a drive up the Chewore River, one of the Zambezi's many tributaries. At this point in the year, the river had long since ceased flowing, but there were still a lot of pools. We didn't expect to see buffalo, or at least I didn't; I think we were looking for an impala for the game scouts' weekly rations. But late in the day, we came around a little bend and spotted six buffalo bulls drinking not much more than two hundred yards away. They heard the vehicle and started drifting slowly into the heavy, riverine cover, stopping to look back every few steps.

One of the bulls towered over his buddies in body size, with horns to match. His bosses were incredible, eighteen-inch bosses that you hear about, but never see. The rest of the horns weren't too bad, a beautiful curl and a spread that had to be in the low forties. The two hundred yards between us was too far for a sensible shot at a buffalo, though hardly impossible with a good .375. And while we were there to make a film about buffalo hunting, I never thought about shooting. We did talk about going after them right then, but only a half-hour of daylight remained. So we left them for the evening, picking up on their tracks at first light.

Hell, we never saw any of them! We got on them just fine, but during the night they had mingled with a small, mixed herd. The first buffalo we saw was a cow—where did she come from? Then a calf. Then another cow. It was impossibly thick—these buffalo were less than ten yards away—and then the inevitable happened, and they exploded. We had followed the wrong group; the wise old bulls stayed in the riverine cover. We figured it out and went back, finding them again readily. But the closest we got was hearing buffalo crashing away, almost at our fingertips. We gave up, hoping to encounter this group again, but we never did.

That one I understand. It was just too darned thick, and we had no chance. There was another good bull that gave me the slip back in '93, but I will never know why. I was hunting in Masailand's famed Mto Wa Mbu block with Geoff Broom. Late one evening, we glassed—how rare is that?—a herd of buffalo on a ridge above the Great Rift Valley. We had to hustle, but we got on them with a bit of daylight to spare. There was one really good bull in the herd, with heavy bosses and maybe forty-four inches wide, his high horn tips distinctively sharp. We saw him several times, but couldn't get a shot in the press of buffalo. Then it started to get dark. No problem, we'd get him in the morning.

Next day, we got on the herd easily. They were up on the ridges, so we glassed them from the bottom (again, how rare is that?), figured an intercept route, and hiked our way up. We got on them just fine and made several approaches, but we never saw that bull. Or any other decent bull. The wind stayed fine, so we kept with them and kept looking. It wasn't all that thick, just enough that we could never see the whole herd, maybe sixty or seventy buffalo, at once.

Eventually, they lay down in some thick vegetation. We crawled this way and that, and just couldn't find him. And now we had a problem. It was past noon, and our water bottles were empty. This was supposed to be a quick hunt, but it would be another three hours before they got up on their own. Too long to wait. We charged into the herd, and they charged out of the cover, then stopped, bunched,

Hunting in the Selous, Art Wheaton and PH Cliff Walker closed nicely on this herd—but just when they were in position for a shot, the herd lay down in the open! There was no choice but to wait them out.

Buffalo may bed for the entire day or they may just take a short rest. The latter is most likely if they're in the open; they will seek shade when sun gets too hot. In this case, after a wait of an hour or so, the herd got up, and Art Wheaton took this fine bull.

and turned to face us, as buffalo will often do. Shoot, he just wasn't there. But he had to be there, didn't he?

When buffalo are lying down, it's very difficult to get close and sort through them. Even if the wind is perfect, some will always be watching and listening. There will be buffalo hidden in thick vegetation that you cannot see, and, in a big herd, there will be thick clumps of bedded buffalo that you cannot see into. Then there are several options to finding your bull.

You can work around this way and that, often crawling while always watching the wind, and try to see them. Being an impatient person, I tend to like this option, but now you are holding that time bomb again, one with a very short fuse. If you get lucky, you might find the bull you're looking for, but you won't do this for very long before you spook the whole mess.

You can get it over with quickly, charging into the herd and spooking them on purpose as Geoff and I did. Sometimes, as those buffalo did, they will stand and give you a look. During the last hour of daylight, this is a very sound tactic, and we'll talk about that in more depth later. At midday, though, when the buffalo are resting peacefully, this is a desperate measure. When they spook, they will probably run far. You might get a shot, but don't count on it.

The best answer, and by far the most difficult for the hunters, is simply to back off a wee bit and wait them out. Sometime within a half-hour of four o'clock they will get up, and then you can work them during those last golden hours of daylight. The problem is that it's usually a long, miserable wait. With luck, you have some water, but you're going to be hot, and the bugs are likely to be really awful.

Tsetse flies are terrible things. Their bite is like a hot needle, and they are incredibly tough. You can slap them so hard that the sting of your own hand remains for seconds, and the insect simply flies away. Still, I just love them. They carry sleeping sickness (only rarely transmitted to humans), so you won't find much livestock in Africa's fast-shrinking tsetse fly country. Everyone has a cause; mine may well be creating the Save The Tsetse Foundation. Mopane bees are another story. These sightless, stingless bees are perfectly harmless, but they congregate around your eyes and ears and nostrils and drive you nuts. Waiting for the buffalo to move is not much fun.

Getting close doesn't mean getting a shot. The presentation must be right, and you must have total confidence. If everything isn't perfect, you must keep working them until you have the shot you want. (Photo taken from the DVD Boddington on Buffalo)

Typically, the professional hunter and client will move forward when contact is made, while the rest of the party stays back a bit to reduce movement and noise as much as possible.

Whether to try to creep in or to wait is not an uncommon decision. It's great if you can catch a herd while they're still moving, but unless you get lucky, the combination of the time to find tracks and the time it takes to follow them means that, much of time, the buffalo will be lying down about the time you catch up. In 2000, I was hunting in the Selous Reserve with hunting partner Art Wheaton of Remington Arms and another young Zimbabwean PH, Cliff Walker. On this day, it was Art's turn. We found tracks in the early midmorning, and we didn't follow for that long before spotting buffalo feeding through an open *dambo*, or meadow. Perfect.

Cliff started to maneuver to get ahead of them, and we had already glimpsed a good bull, when the darned things started to lie down. Our bull was in the middle of a big group, lying like cattle in a little open space. We crept up to maybe eighty yards and glassed them. Yes, there was our bull, easily forty inches wide with broad bosses, and totally blocked by a mass of buffalo.

In this case, it was too early for them to be bedded up for the day, and as the sun got higher, there was no way they would stay in the open and bake. I guess they just wanted to stop and chew their cuds for a little while. So we got all set up and waited. A half-hour later, they started to get up. When Art's bull stood and got clear, he walloped him, and that was that.

Often the wait is longer. It was the same safari, but another last day. I had one more buffalo on license, and that was our mission. We got onto a nice herd fairly early in the morning, about nine o'clock. The tracks were reasonably fresh, and I guess we followed for about two hours. It was a big herd, and when we caught up, some of them were up in *miombo* forest to our right, while the bulk of the herd was scattered in an open donga, still feeding, but clearly concentrated in the shade of some scattered trees.

This was not a day to be especially picky. We found a reasonable bull, very mature and hard-bossed, with good configuration, but clearly somewhere in the upper thirties for spread. Fine. But there were quite a few buffalo to the right and left and between him and us, and while we were still trying to figure all this out, the darned things started to lie down. We were totally stuck. The bull we wanted was probably a hundred fifty yards away, a very long shot, but practical with the

Working your way through the brush and then getting a shot is almost always a critical problem—and often the vegetation will be too thick to shoot. (Photo by Dave Fulson)

Getting close means spending a lot of time trying to sort out black forms in dark shadow. Chances are the buffalo will spook before you figure them all out, but that's just part of the game. (Photo taken from the DVD *Boddington on Buffalo*)

scoped .375 Remington Ultra Magnum I was carrying. But he lay down in a mass of buffalo on the far side of a stout acacia; there were lots of buffalo between him and us. It was much too far to charge into them (we'd have buffalo all over us, but we'd never see him again), and out of maybe two hundred buffalo we could see, he was the only shootable bull. We had two choices, either walk away or wait.

Five hours. We waited five hours and a bit of change. It was a very hot day, and I don't think they started to get up until half past four. We had the scant shade of one little tree among us, and the mopane bees were terrible. But we knew, sooner or later, they would get up. In this case, it was later, and our group with the bull in it got up last of all. That made things very exciting, but it was the buffalo in the trees to our right, getting up first, that really made things interesting: They started feeding right toward us.

Undisturbed, buffalo really aren't dangerous at all, unless, of course, you run into a cow with a young calf. So, that is what happened. A very young calf trotted right toward us with her very big mother right behind. I saw Cliff snake his .577 double to him. At this point, the calf wasn't thirty feet away, and its mom not much farther. But I had to ignore them, they were Cliff's problem. My problem was our bull, which had just gotten up. He was standing behind the tree, covered. But he had to step out—provided, of course, we didn't have buffalo all over us before he did.

This would be the longest shot I have ever taken on a buffalo. I got into a target sitting position, legs crossed, with a tight sling wrapped around my arm. Cliff's big .577 was a great comfort as I turned my back on the buffalo bearing down on us from the right. Timing is everything. My buffalo stepped out just before Cliff had to do something about that little calf and his not-so-little mom. I shot the bull on the shoulder, and while he lurched into the running mass, we had buffalo running everywhere. Fortunately, they all ran the other direction. A few minutes later, we found my bull standing, sick, in a grassy donga, and I finished him there.

Circling and Cutting

The ideal situation is to close on a moving herd. They are not unaware, not at all, but because their primary focus is grazing, and because their own movement masks both your movement and your noise (nothing will mask your scent), this is the usual tactic. The goal is to look over as many bulls as you can without spooking the herd. The difficulty grows exponentially with the number of buffalo.

It's easy to say that the older bulls will be trailing the rear of the group, and this is most likely if they're actually moving. If they're simply feeding along—which is what you really want—placement of the bulls within the herd is much more random. So you want to look at the whole herd. If you can. Wind direction remains the key. If the stars are in alignment (not to mention the wind), you simply circle around and get in front of the herd, then let them all pass. I'm not sure I've ever seen it work quite this perfectly.

More frequently, the wind is an issue, there's too much cover, and sometimes there are just too many buffalo to see them all. A buffalo herd is quite spread out as it feeds along. When tracking,

Although buffalo have very keen eyesight, their sense of smell is their first line of defense. As long as you have some cover and move very slowly, you can usually close within shooting distance, but if and only if the wind is in your favor.

the trackers must focus on a single track or group of tracks, but the whole group may be spread across a front of several hundred yards. Once you get past two or three, it is actually quite rare to know exactly how many buffalo you are following until you see them. So, when tracking, you will hit the group at a certain point—maybe the front, maybe the rear, maybe in the middle. Andrew Dawson calls it "cutting."

Maybe you see no bulls at all, or maybe the bulls you do see aren't any good. Now the task is to see the rest of them. The wind dictates what you can do. Sometimes you must try to circle the entire herd. Sometimes you must cut to the front, and sometimes you must cut to the rear. Using their ash bags, watching the wind every step, the trackers will take you away from the herd, then back into it in a semicircle, which becomes a series of semicircles as you make multiple cuts, trying to see them all.

As always, you are carrying that time bomb. Sooner or later, one of several things will happen. You will be satisfied that you've seen all the bulls and none are worthy (rare!); you find the bull you're looking for (not quite so rare); or something gives you away and you start all over (most common). The thicker the cover or the more fickle the wind, the more likely that time bomb is to explode.

In 1998, I was hunting in the Zambezi Valley with Swarovski's Jim Morey, outfitter Russ Broom, and professional hunter Rory Muil. This would be Jim's first buffalo, and we found the fresh, fresh tracks of "his" herd crossing a road in the late morning. In fact, it was so late that, despite the freshness, I figured they would be bedded before we hit them. Not so. We caught the tail of the herd an hour later in an incredibly brushy valley, then scrambled up the steep side to get ahead. Had it been a bit more open it would have been very easy. We would have monitored the progress of the herd by the cattle sounds and the dust they were raising, but what we had was *miombo* so thick, we could only make out the occasional shape.

We leapfrogged ahead, using rocky ledges and brush ant heaps as vantage points, but this went on for a long time, and we still had no idea how many buffalo we were dealing with, nor whether there were any good bulls in the herd. Finally, they tired of the thick bottom and started climbing out the opposite bank. We were perched on an ant heap maybe two hundred yards away and could see them all as they clambered out. Yes, there were some nice bulls in there—but it was too far. So Rory cut again, circling out around the herd, and this time we caught them in more open cover on the far side of the valley. Jim made a nice shot with his Dakota .375, and that was the end of that buffalo hunt.

Big Herds or *Dugga* Boys?
Chapter 6

Serious buffalo hunters have a longstanding disagreement over whether you're better off hunting a big herd or a small group of bachelor bulls. Folks, you don't always have a choice. I've been in a lot of places where I was just happy to *have* buffalo to follow, *any* buffalo. It's rare to have the luxury to decide whether you're going to follow big herds or just look for the tracks of a few big-footed, outcast bulls. But whether you have the choice or not, there are big differences between hunting a big herd and hunting a small group of bachelor bulls.

On the surface, it might seem that the latter is easier. You know they are bulls, and you know there won't be as many eyes, ears, and noses to deal with. All true, but it isn't quite that easy. Following a big herd is very, very simple. It takes only a modest amount of tracking skill to follow the spoor of a large number of buffalo. The grass will be beaten down by their passage. There will be lots of dung, and even on the hardest ground, you can find scuff marks and stones displaced by hooves. It's very much a numbers game. Following just a few buffalo, on the other hand, can be very difficult, depending on the soil and vegetation. Following just one or two buffalo is serious tracking, and only the very best can do it.

I am convinced that the very best African trackers can follow darn near anything over almost any surface. But tracks are very hard to follow in dry grass or over hard, sun-baked, or stony ground. Especially today, with fewer Africans really living on the land, real tracking is becoming a lost art. Some are better than others, but tracking just a few buffalo takes a high level of both skill and experience. The smaller the group of buffalo, the slower the tracking will be (which also has the downfall of making it later in the day when you make contact). Too, the smaller the group, the greater the possibility that the tracks will be utterly lost. This can happen at any time, especially in areas where there is a lot of grass—and if it happens a few hours along on the track, then that valuable hunting day is lost.

Let's say, however, that your trackers are among the very best and that your PH has confidence that they can follow the spoor wherever it leads. Hunting days are still precious, so the discussion then falls to where the best chances lie in finding the kind of buffalo you're looking for. Should you pass up the tracks of a few bulls and keep looking for a larger group? Or should you pass up the clear spoor of a big herd and continue the search for a few big bulls' tracks? Let's look at the likely composition of both.

Herd Bulls

Buffalo herds are usually comprised of both sexes and almost all age groups. The herd size varies widely. The largest herd I have ever seen was in Zambia's Kafue region in 1984. They moved in close-by our camp in the night, and we could hear them bellowing and shifting. In the morning, it was a simple matter to find them. We could no longer hear them, but a long *dambo* near camp was literally flattened. No real tracking was required. We simply strolled along in their wake until we came upon them. There was no counting this herd, a black mass of buffalo across a front of several hundred feet, with depth beyond our vision. I'm sure they numbered at least five hundred, and could have been many more. I have seen herds almost this large in the Selous Reserve, as well.

In areas where there are lots of buffalo, I don't think a herd this size is unusual, but most of the "big" herds I have encountered seem to number perhaps a couple hundred animals. What I think of as "small" herds might run from a very modest group of twenty up to perhaps sixty or eighty animals. Regardless of size, you know that a herd will be comprised mostly of cows, usually with plenty of calves at heel. You can also bet, almost universally, that any herd will also

I took this typical herd bull with Andrew Dawson in the Zambezi Valley in 2004. He is fully mature with good, hard bosses, but his horn tips are long and sharp and have not yet begun to wear.

have at least a few bulls and that most of them will be young. Beyond that, there's no telling what else you might find.

"Herd" bulls are more likely to be younger bulls than old-timers. Middle-aged bulls, perhaps seven to ten years old, seem to do most of the breeding, and there will usually be some of these within any herd. Bulls like this are likely to have almost complete horn development, possessing whatever horn spread they are going to develop, probably with long, sharp, horn tips. Depending entirely on their genetics, they may also have extremely wide (or narrow) bosses. Unfortunately, few of the bulls in this age class will have formed the completely hard bosses that most hunters look for in trophy buffalo.

It is also unlikely that a herd will have any really old, outcast bulls. The real old-timers tend to go off on their own, perhaps with a few other old gentlemen. However, in that long period between sexual maturity and senility, most bulls will travel with herds at least some of the time. This is probably especially true in the weeks after the rainy season, when most cows come in season, but I have seen good, hard-bossed trophy bulls in herds at almost any time of the year. Also at any time of the year, I've spent a lot of time combing through herds without seeing any fully mature males. So, the good news is that any given herd, at any given time, may have a few genuine, fully mature, hard-bossed bulls. The bad news is that any given herd, at any given time, may not. Again, to some extent, it's a numbers game. Any herd, of any size, *may* hold the bull of your dreams—but it's almost certain that a herd running up into the hundreds will have at least a few mature bulls traveling with them.

Dugga Boys

Now to the boys' clubs. As I mentioned earlier, there are bachelor herds and there are *dugga* boys. Males of most species (including ours), like to get away from the noise and hubbub of the women and kids. "*Dugga* boys" has become sort of a catchphrase these days to denote any bachelor group. This is misuse of the term, because you will often find young bulls, years from true trophy status, traveling with other young bulls. True *dugga* boys, the mud bulls, are older, outcast bulls. They will have hard bosses and, thus, are

True dugga *boys do come and go out of mixed herds, especially when cows are in season. This huge-bodied and very old buffalo was taken out of a big herd, while I was hunting with PH Paddy Curtis in the Selous Reserve.*

PH Ronnie MacFarlane (left) and Jack Atcheson Jr. with a classic dugga boy. His tips are worn and his boss has started to crack and peel away, a real old warrior. A buffalo like this may not score especially well, but he's a great trophy.

shootable bulls by my standards. But, that doesn't mean they are trophy bulls by record-book standards. A true *dugga* boy is old, up into his teens. He lives a solitary and fairly sedentary life, sometimes alone, though often in the company of a few chums. While he will surely have fully hard bosses, it is almost as sure that his horn tips will have worn down—sometimes all the way to the bases. Broken horns are common.

Bachelor groups, which come and go and mix into the herds, could be comprised of anything. I have seen bachelor herds that were all young bulls, and once, in Botswana, I saw three bachelor bulls accompanied by a half-grown calf. Go figure! So big bull tracks don't necessarily mean *old* bulls, and old bulls aren't automatically large trophies. To some extent, it's a matter of playing the odds, and it depends on what you're looking for.

A small group of big-footed bulls is likely to be genuine *dugga* boys. Remember that one or two sets of tracks can be very difficult to follow. Weighed against this is the fact that old bulls generally don't like to travel great distances between good grazing, water, and security cover. They don't need as much grass as a large herd, nor as much water. So you can probably catch up to them fairly quickly, and with only a few sets of nostrils, eyes, and ears, your chances of seeing what's there and maneuvering for a shot are very good.

Playing the Odds

Your goals come into play here. Are you looking for any mature bull? Then you might want to take a chance that your trackers can hold a small number of tracks, because once you make contact, the fewer the buffalo, the better your chances of both looking at them all and getting a shot. On the other hand, if you're seriously looking for the best bull you can find in the time you have available, you need to give your hunt some serious thought.

If I'm trying to find a good bull, I don't personally like to follow just two or three bull tracks, because in my experience, the odds are against you. Unless the wind goes funky or you make a mistake, chances are you will close with them and get a look. But trophy buffalo that have hard bosses *and* good spread *and* nice

Typical dugga *boys in the Zambezi Valley. All these bulls are of a type: Heavy-bossed, fully mature, and very average in width. It's a numbers game. The more bulls you can follow, the better your chances of a good one, but it's never a sure thing.*

conformation don't grow on trees. Absent really good luck, you need to look at quite a few buffalo to find one that has it all. Thus, the smaller the group you're following, the less likelihood such a bull will be among them.

I mentioned that very short buffalo hunt in Zambia. It was July, very early in most Kafue areas. There is still plenty of water in the adjoining Kafue National Park, and, at this time, that's where most of the herd animals, including buffalo, can be found. Out in our hunting block, Mulobezi, there were a few scattered water holes, and many of them had *dugga* boys hanging around. We found the large, fresh tracks of just one bull, and under the circumstances, my PH, Russ Broom, elected to follow. The circumstances were: There weren't many buffalo in the area; and this time I wasn't looking for a huge bull. I'd have been perfectly delighted if the tracks led to a fifty-inch buffalo, but our plan was to make the most expeditious buffalo hunt we could, then head up to Bangweulu, so we could devote as much time as possible to hunting sitatunga. I told him I'd be happy with any mature buffalo bull that would look good in a magazine article!

So we followed the abnormally large tracks of a single bull, and an hour later we found him sleeping. He was, indeed, abnormally big in the body, and he was old, with wonderfully thick bosses. The rest of his horns were thick, with worn tips, but other than making sure neither horn was broken, we didn't look very hard. When he got up, I took a good, slightly quartering-away shot at him with a single-shot .375 Dakota. He ran a couple dozen yards and fell over, and the next morning early, we were on our way to Bangweulu.

On numerous occasions, I have seen solitary *dugga* boys; you often encounter them in the late morning and afternoon in shady spots along sand rivers. But I think that was one of very few times that I have followed a single bull. Most of the time, your PH and trackers will nix the idea, simply because too much time will be expended with only a small chance of finding a good bull at the end of the track.

Math wasn't my strongest subject, but it seems logical to me that *two* bull tracks double the chances of seeing good horns. This

My old friend and Kenya PH Willem van Dyk tries to work out a track. Deciding whether or not to follow a given spoor is one of the PH's most difficult decisions. He cannot predict what might happen, but he will not want to take a track unless he's pretty sure you can catch up (and there is a reasonable chance of seeing a good trophy).

Most good-size herds will have at least a couple of mature bulls somewhere in the press. The problem with herds is always getting a look at all the bulls because there are so many eyes, ears, and noses—and so many other buffalo in the way.

may be true, but for many professional hunters, this still isn't enough—especially early in a hunt, before you might have learned that at this particular time, buffalo are a bit scarce. Remember, aside from trophy potential, there is also the difficulty in holding the tracks of so small a number. On many occasions, I've had professional hunters decline to follow two sets of big tracks. Years ago I was perplexed, even frustrated, by this. After all, I was here to hunt buffalo bulls, and there were fresh tracks. So let's go! Now I understand it all a whole lot better, and it comes down to this: Provided you've chosen him with appropriate care, your professional hunter won't be right all the time, but he will understand how to best play the odds and how to best utilize your hunting days far better than you!

I was in the Mulobezi again just a year later, in 1996, also with Russ Broom. By this time, Zambia had changed from a more or less "open ticket" to requiring specific hunting licenses to be purchased in advance. I had intended to hunt leopard and wanted a roan, but beyond that, I only had licenses for buffalo (of course!) and a few bait animals—impala, warthog, zebra. This hunt was in September, when much of the water within the national park has dried up and the Kafue hunting blocks really start to come alive. The rains had been heavy that year, so this process was a bit behind schedule. Actually, there was still a lot of water everywhere! There were plenty of sable, eland, hartebeest, zebra, and the common species in our area. But roan were just starting to move in, and buffalo herds were scarce at the outset of the safari.

We had a huge screwup, and a leopard license was not available. Unfilled licenses from previous clients could be transferred, so, as a consolation prize, Russ offered me an eland permit. Great! Except that we took a huge bull on the first day, and it was no trick to take any of the common animals on any given day. So we spent our time looking for buffalo and roan, both of which were damn hard to come by, a situation we hoped was temporary. The roan was just a matter of checking some of the best areas. Toward the end of the hunt, they did indeed start to move in, and both Bob Petersen and I took nice bulls at the tail end. Later on, the buffalo also moved in, but during the first few days, it was much like the previous year: All we had to work with was a few resident *dugga* boys scattered here and there. This time it was complicated by the fact that, with plenty of time available, I wanted to look for a good bull!

We followed a few small groups, closing with some and turning them down, losing the tracks of others in the plentiful tall grass. Late one morning, mostly because we had absolutely nothing else going, we followed the tracks of two bulls. They took us quite a long distance, and with so many patches of unburned grass, it was an extremely laborious and time-consuming job. Eventually, they led into a nasty thicket of small trees, almost like a forest of picket fences one after another. By now the wind had become unstable, and we jumped them about four times before giving it up.

Among all the tracking jobs, this one was memorable for two reasons. First, at one stage we got a good look at them as they galloped straight away through the trees. One bull was unremarkable enough that I don't recall him at all. The second bull was one of the big boys, heavy-bossed and, although fairly flat-horned, wonderfully wide. I have been exceptionally lucky with big

Another Botswana dugga boy, old, with well-worn horns. Even though bulls like this don't "score" particularly well, many professional hunters consider them the finest of buffalo trophies because they are past breeding.

buffalo, so this one stands out as one of the best bulls to give me the slip while I've been hunting these great bovines.

The second thing that stands out is that we humans always wonder how buffalo—or any horned or antlered animal—manage to slip through incredibly thick vegetation with that headgear projecting on either side. I don't recall which time it was that we bumped them and they rattled away, but one time, when we resumed tracking, we found where the bull had passed exactly and precisely between two stout trees, leaving the bark smeared on both sides by the passage of the outer curve of his horns! Do they know with that much precision just how much clearance they need? Had we any question about just how wide that bull really was, those marks gave us the answer.

Safety in Numbers?

The larger the group of bulls, the better the odds of finding a good one, but this is also quite random. Earlier I told about that "longest tracking job," that group of a dozen or so bulls we tracked in the Selous

Reserve. There should have been a couple of really good bulls in a group that size, but there was not. The bull we took was a perfectly acceptable bull and, perhaps, a great "last day" bull, but he was a long way from being a monster.

Still, most groups of, say, three or four or, even better, a half-dozen bulls (whether bachelor bulls or true *dugga* boys), should have at least one bull that's better than his fellow companions. In the Zambezi Valley, in '98, I took a very nice bull—big bosses, good curve, spread of forty-two inches—out of a group of three *dugga* boys. My first "really big bull," taken in Zambia, in 1984, came out of a bachelor group of maybe four or five bulls. Yet we never saw them all, let alone counted them. This one had wonderful bosses and a spread in the mid-forties, and we shot him the instant we saw him!

But you never know. In 2004, hunting in the Zambezi Valley with Andrew Dawson, we were cruising a sand river in midmorning, specifically looking for buffalo tracks and, in this area, expecting to find where *dugga* boys had crossed. I think it was about nine o'clock, and we had seen many tracks from "yesterday." Tracks in the sand are especially difficult to age, but we'd had some unusually strong winds, so blown-in leaves were conspicuous. Finally, we found the fresh tracks of a couple of bulls and we took to them.

Again, it isn't unusual to be uncertain about exactly how many tracks you are following. Nor, once you get past one or two, does it really matter—the more the merrier! Andrew's trackers, Mukasa and Lummock, were as good as any I have ever seen. Not long after taking the tracks, they reported there were three bulls. Even better! We caught them in a little donga choked with thick, low, mopane scrub, still feeding, but preparing to lie down. The two bulls we could see were sort of normal, mature, *dugga* boys, nearly identical, with about thirty-seven inches of spread. By the time we figured this out, they were all lying down, nearly invisible though we were barely sixty yards away. The wind was steady in our faces, and we needed to see that last one. Andrew figured it was open enough for a shot when they all stood, which, absent human scent, they would most likely do when they finally heard us approaching.

So we stalked right into them, and they got up at less than twenty yards. Except there were four bulls, not three. The odds were there,

Zimbabwean PH Angie Angelloz and I followed a couple of dugga boys through some really thick stuff in Zambia's Kafue region. One was a great bull, and one of the times we jumped him he barked these trees with the outer curve of his horns, showing us just how wide he was. Unfortunately, we never got a shot!

but the big horns were not. All of them were virtually identical, heavy-horned with bosses that were fully hard but quite average in width and all in the thirty-six- to thirty-seven-inch range. We got some great video footage of them at point-blank range, and again when they scrambled up the far side of the donga and turned back to look at us. And that's where we left them. I think it was two days later that we tracked just two *dugga* boys and took the kind of bull we'd been looking for, a wonderfully heavy old-timer with beautiful, forty-inch horns.

Given a choice, I think you would always follow a bachelor group of three or more bulls. Most of the time they will be of the fully mature, hard-bossed age class you are looking for. Perhaps more importantly, you will probably close on them without spending a lot of hours on the track. And most important of all, you will probably be able to see them all, or at least most of them, and make up your mind. You don't always, or even very often, have such a choice.

Because they travel less and because the tracks are harder to spot, it is much more difficult to find the spoor of just a few buffalo bulls, whereas large herds leave more tracks over a much greater area.

In the Herds

All told, I have spent much more time working larger mixed herds than I have following bachelor groups. Also, although this perhaps naturally follows from the previous assertion, I have shot many more buffalo from herds than I have from bachelor groups. I don't know about your hunting goals, but remember that mine have varied widely from safari to safari. Always the goal has been to take a mature bull, but often I've been short on time or more in the mode to hunt other species, or I have been more interested in testing a rifle or cartridge or bullet. So I guess you can say that I'm always looking for the best bull I can find under the circumstances—but that doesn't mean I'm always trophy hunting.

On my first trip to Tanzania, in 1988, the trip was split with ten days in Masailand, and ten days in the Selous. In Masailand, I was looking for one of those wide-horned, East African bulls we all dream about. We looked over a lot of buffalo and turned down a number of bulls, but I never fired a shot at a buffalo. Thus, when we got to the Selous, I still had three buffalo on license. I could afford not to be quite so picky!

Early in the hunt, we tracked up a nice herd while they were still feeding in open *miombo* forest. Typical of a feeding herd, we saw black shapes moving at the limit of our vision. My PH, Paddy Curtis, immediately shifted to the left to get completely downwind, and we quickly caught up with the tail end of the herd. There was a mature bull with a monstrous body and thick, worn horns, and I shot him without hesitation. Maybe there were better bulls, maybe there weren't. Maybe we could have seen them or maybe we would have spooked the whole mess. But on this day, at this stage of the hunt, it was time to shoot a buffalo. With that mindset, your chances of shooting a mature bull out of a herd are very good. If your goals are higher, or if it's your intention to look at each and every bull before deciding, then it gets exponentially more difficult. As I look back, it's fair to say that my very best bulls have come from bachelor groups. On the other hand, I have taken some very good bulls out of herds.

Hunting in herds, I have seen a whole bunch of bulls that, at first glance, had wonderfully wide, beautifully formed horns. On close inspection, most of these have needed another year or two to be fully mature. Part and parcel to hunting big herds is that you will see a lot of immature bulls. You will also follow herds—and shoot bulls out of them—without ever being certain you've seen them all. Better stated, actually, is that most of the time, whether you shoot or not, you will come away very certain that you didn't see them all!

The bigger the herd, the more difficult it is to sort through all the bulls. There is a point up to, say, forty or fifty animals, where, depending on the cover and how long the wind and your luck hold, you have a pretty good chance of seeing all the bulls. Unfortunately, since to some extent it is a numbers game, with small herds there's a strong likelihood that you can see all the bulls without seeing a

Herds are easy to follow, but it's very difficult to sort through them to see all the bulls. Chances are you will spook them before you see them all, yet another part of the game. (Photo taken from the DVD *Boddington on Buffalo*)

Dave Fulson with a classic dugga *boy, taken in the Zambezi Valley. The tips are worn, the spread is average, and the bosses are heavy. There won't be much record-book score, but an old bull like this is a great trophy.* (Photo by Dave Fulson)

single shootable animal. With larger groups, it becomes increasingly unlikely that you'll see them all. Sometimes this doesn't matter. The search ends when you find the kind of bull that pleases you, and you'll never know, or much care, whether there was a better bull in the group. Or it ends when it ends. The herd crosses into a park, or when you've had enough for one day, or when you've spooked them so many times they're completely on edge and further pursuit seems pointless.

Exactly when this end point is reached varies infinitely depending on how much pressure the buffalo have been subjected to, what the wind is doing, and even on the terrain. In relatively open country, you might be able to stay with a herd most of the day, but if you have to work in close, they will eventually get your scent, and you won't do this many times before they're too edgy to approach at all. But, sometimes it's amazing what you can get away with.

When Ed Weatherby introduced his .416 Weatherby Magnum in the late '80s, I accompanied him to northeastern Botswana's Chobe area to try it out on buffalo. We didn't allocate a lot of time—probably not enough, under the circumstances. At that particular time there was quite a lot of perfectly legal, resident hunting pressure in that area. Buffalo were hard to find, and they were quite spooky.

One morning we found the very fresh tracks of a large herd that had apparently just left the flood plain and entered the mopane forest. We followed along, and although it took a while to sort out a bull and get a shot, the wind was favorable and we never spooked them. They were feeding their way along quietly, and it was open enough that we were able to maneuver to the side of the herd and work our way in and out without spooking them. Eventually, we caught a nice bull on our side of the herd, sort of a typical Botswana bull with heavy bosses and a normal spread in the upper thirties.

This was actually the first time I ever used a pure lung shot on a buffalo. He was standing with his belly and lower shoulder obscured by grass, and the front part of his shoulder was obscured by a small tree. With a scoped rifle and a good rest, I shot him very carefully tight behind the shoulder, just under the horizontal halfway point. The buffalo around him exploded and charged deeper into the mopane, and there was no chance for a second shot. He ran maybe

A face-to-face encounter with an old bull. We were trying to get a closer look at three dugga boys we'd been tracking, when a fourth, unseen bull came out of nowhere. He wasn't what we were looking for, so we had a standoff for a few seconds, and then he turned and joined his buddies. (Photo taken from the DVD Boddington on Buffalo)

sixty yards and went down, and this was one of few times that I haven't fired an insurance shot. When we approached, we could see him clearly and also where the bullet had struck, so instead of shooting, the trackers threw some sticks. There was no reaction. The bull was completely finished.

So, we had taken him with just one shot and very minimal disturbance. Ed Weatherby still needed a bull. Our professional hunter, Steve Liversedge, suggested we should leave one of the trackers with my bull to claim ownership, while the rest of us continued after the herd. I didn't think there was much point, but I still had a lot to learn. We made contact again in less than an hour, and after a bit more maneuvering, Ed took an almost identical bull, his with a frontal shot that, from his superfast new cartridge, nearly flattened the bull on the spot!

This was a very large herd. Spread out in the mopane the way they were, I have no idea how many animals it contained. Even though we took two nice bulls from the herd with relative ease, I'm certain we never saw all of the bulls, and we may not have even seen a fraction of them. Maybe there were some real monsters in there, and maybe there weren't. The tantalizing thing about working big herds, whether you end it with a shot or not, is that you almost always walk away wondering.

Eyes and Ears Open
Chapter 7

So you're looking for tracks—big herds, *dugga* boys, both, just so they're fresh enough to follow. The search might take minutes, hours, or days, and there isn't much you can do to help. This part is all up to your professional hunter and his trackers. They will probably have pretty good notions of where to look, but only the buffalo determine where they will place their spoor. You will probably cruise endlessly along dirt tracks, where buffalo movement is likely. In some areas, you will grind in low gear, tires half-deflated, along miles of sand rivers, and you might walk quite a few miles of these dry riverbeds on foot. You will certainly check water holes, some that you can drive to, and others that you must walk to.

During any and all of these activities, it is always possible, and sometimes likely, that you will see buffalo. To see buffalo without tracking, you have to be in the right place at the right time, but just how likely this is depends a lot on density, not only of the cover, but that of the buffalo, as well. If the cover restricts your visibility to a few yards off the hunting track (like that of the floor of the Zambezi Valley), it takes a whole lot of luck to actually see buffalo without tracking, but it sometimes happens. Where the cover is more open, then, as you move through likely areas at the right time of day, you are increasingly likely to see buffalo. In hilly country that offers some visibility, like the hills of Masailand, and the ridges that lead to the Zambezi's escarpment, you might even glass for buffalo.

Once in a while you hit an area that has such a concentration of buffalo that you just plain run into them. In 2000, I hunted in

Swanepoel & Scandrol's block in the western Selous, not far from the beginning of the Kilombero Valley. Buffalo are so plentiful in the Selous that during my three hunts there I have always seen a lot of buffalo, even in thick vegetation. This particular area was ridiculous. We didn't run into buffalo every day, although every day we ran into tracks we could follow. But in the course of an "average" hunting day, we would actually see buffalo two or three times.

As I've said, this is normally just a starting point. If it's fairly open and you see buffalo at a couple of hundred yards, you can't shoot, but you might well begin a stalk without doing any tracking at all. If they move off at the approach of the vehicle, you at least have a known point to begin tracking and, more importantly, knowledge of the exact time they passed through. You don't want to miss the experience of tracking buffalo, so don't be too upset if you don't see bull after bull standing alongside the road. But while your professional hunter and his trackers are studying that same road for fresh tracks, it pays to pay attention. Likewise, when you are tracking: Anyone can see the buffalo first.

Listen

One of the big differences between *dugga* boys and mixed herds is that the former are relatively silent, while the latter are downright noisy. Oh, if the wind catches you from behind, either way you'll hear brush crack and hoof beats dying away, but I'm not talking about that. Buffalo in herds are extremely vocal, especially while moving, feeding, and watering. *Dugga* boys pretty much keep their counsel whatever they're doing.

In thick cover, you will usually hear a buffalo herd long before you see them. Yes, they sound just like cattle, lowing and snorting and bellowing. It's a wonderful sound, and on several occasions I've lain awake in my tent listening to buffalo passing by or watering in the dark. Once you've heard buffalo a couple of times, you will never mistake them for anything else.

The sounds are distinctly bovine, and as you close on a herd, you can bet your PH and his trackers are listening carefully.

In really dry conditions, a herd of buffalo will raise a noticeable dust cloud, even when moving slowly. When they run, you can see the cloud for miles!

Unfortunately, while their ability to see game in the bush probably far exceeds yours and mine, they all have the same hearing problems we do caused by all too many magnums fired next to their ears. Yet they still have the advantage there, which is the same as with visual clues: They know what to listen for, and you do not. Listen anyway, because your hearing, long insulated by earmuffs and plugs, may well be better than theirs!

If you can't yet see them, is it important to hear them? You bet! As you approach buffalo, the more advance notice you can get, the better off you are. You are following a herd along just a few sets of tracks, but buffalo often spread out over a considerable front while moving and feeding, and they move, both in small groups and singles, at different speeds. There might be buffalo to the right or left that you don't know about, so the farther away you can positively locate the herd, the better off you are. Unless the wind is really tricky, the trackers will generally follow directly on the tracks until contact is made. Once you know exactly where the buffalo are, whether from sound or sight, the tracks are forgotten, and the hunt proceeds based on wind direction first and available concealment second.

In thick cover, it is often amazing how close you must be to buffalo before you can see them. You might well be within fifty yards—or half that—of dozens of the great black beasts, yet still be absolutely unable to see them at all. Sound is thus extremely important, not only their snorting and bellowing, which is exasperatingly intermittent, but also the sounds of their movement as they feed along. As you get really close, you'll hear branches crack and footfalls as they shift back and forth. These clues, along with the stomach rumbling and soft movement of ears, are much more prevalent and important with elephant hunting, but you will hear them as you get close to a buffalo herd, and the sounds will often guide your movement.

What you don't want to hear, but sooner or later undoubtedly will, is a great crashing of brush and pounding of hooves when the buffalo sense your presence and spook. Depending on which way it's going, this can be the most frightening racket you will ever hear or, after hours of tracking, the most disheartening. Either way, it's extremely important.

While unprovoked charges are rare, they do occur. If the sound is coming toward you, maybe you can get out of the way, and maybe you can't. But you'd better be ready to try—now! More frequently, what happens in thick cover is that buffalo will catch a bit of human scent on a stray wind swirl or eddy. Although sometimes it seems that way, the animals are not clairvoyant. They can only react in accordance to what their senses tell them. Their normal reaction upon scenting humans is to stampede the other direction, and this is the certain result if the wind really changes on you.

In the case of a stray puff of breeze, they don't always know where the scent came from. They will almost always stampede, but it might be in any direction, including right over the top of you. If the crashing comes toward you, the best course is to get out of the way, but this might only be possible if you have enough warning. If not, find a stout tree to get behind—and be ready! Often, especially if it's just a stray breeze and they can't determine its direction of origin, they will stop short and mill about after a mad dash of a few dozen yards. Provided you don't

Most good buffalo country also has a lot of elephant, so it isn't uncommon to run into elephant when tracking buffalo. So long as you have plenty of standoff distance, it's great to see them—but in thick vegetation, you must always be cautious.

get run over in the process, this may provide a chance to look them over.

So long as you aren't running into their path, you can move with some impunity while they are moving (you won't make nearly as much noise as they do). Upon hearing that crashing, most professional hunters experienced with buffalo will run to the sound, hoping to catch them and get a good look when they stop. It's exciting and, in the heat of the day, downright strenuous. But be careful: If they're truly uncertain about what spooked them and where it came from, after that short stop to get their bearings, they're just as likely to reverse direction and come charging right back along the same path!

Unfortunately, this apparent indecisiveness doesn't happen all that often. Most of the time buffalo know exactly what they're doing, and all that crashing and thundering is very directional. You run to the sound, hoping for a look, but mostly all you see is a press of black bodies and a cloud of lingering dust. Then the sound dies away, and you pull up short to catch your breath. More tracking lies ahead, and now the buffalo know you're behind them.

Look

In the open, it's extremely easy to see buffalo. They're black, they're huge, and there are often lots of them. As I've said, it is amazing how difficult it is to see them in close cover, especially when they're standing still. When they move it gets easier, but by then, it's often too late.

Without actually spotting buffalo, there are a few visual clues available that can indicate their whereabouts. Birds can give them away, and buffalo will raise dust when they're moving. Most buffalo hunting is done during the dry season, when there's plenty of dust to be had. Even one buffalo will raise a considerable dust cloud as he gallops away, but by then, it's too late to help. A small number of buffalo normally won't raise enough dust to notice while they're moving normally and feeding, but a big herd definitely will.

When you're making contact with a herd, you might well hear them up ahead, but if it's a big herd, you will almost certainly see their dust. As with their sound, this enables you to shift from the track to work the herd directly with the wind at its very best. As you maneuver, the dust is often your most important guide. When working a really big herd, hell, the dust is *all* you need to worry about: You know there are buffalo right under the front of the cloud. That day Russ Broom and I worked that huge herd in Zambia, their plume of dust rose like smoke from a forest fire. We never paid attention to tracks or anything else, instead spending our time trying to get the wind right so we could get to the beginning of the dust cloud. Success was limited, because there were just too many buffalo!

Dust can also be especially useful after you've spooked a herd. Bachelor bulls tend to know the game and will often go hard and straight after they've been spooked. A mixed herd, on the other hand, will probably not go very far. The cows have calves to worry about, so unless they're pressed really hard, they will usually

When Swarovski Optik's Jim Morey got his first buffalo in 1999, we were able to monitor the progress of the herd by the dust cloud. They were in really thick vegetation with no buffalo visible, but the dust made it easy to circle and cut back into the herd until he got a shot.

charge away for a short distance, then stop and regroup, sometimes standing for a considerable time before marching away at a more sedate pace. Watch the dust and get to where it stops as quickly as you can.

Dust clouds can also initiate a hunt, if you're paying attention. In '94, I was hunting in the Selous Reserve in Luke Samaras' blocks; his son, Jasper, was guiding me. I don't recall the time of day, but I think it was late morning. Much of the soil there is red clay, and we were driving along when, at about the same time, both of us saw a huge plume of red dust just a couple of hundred yards off the track. I don't know who said it first, either, but the word sprang almost instantly to our tongues: "Buffalo!"

Maybe we would have found their tracks right around the next bend, but we didn't follow any tracks. Jasper stopped the truck, and we grabbed our rifles and followed the dust. It took a little while to come up on the herd, and then it took more time to work them. They were just moving and feeding, but it was thick, and there were a lot of buffalo. We got within maybe seventy-five yards and climbed up on a big red ant heap, hoping to glass the herd. That was where one of those stray eddies caught us, and a wall of buffalo bore down on us in an instant. I was thankful for the ant heap!

As they passed, there was a good bull on our side of the herd, very close. I was hunting with Paul Roberts, then proprietor of the John Rigby company, and this was the first use of his brand-new .450 Rigby Rimless Magnum. Paul and I were both sort of competing to see who would take the first buffalo with it, so as this bull came by, I shot him on the shoulder with a Woodleigh softpoint, then put another one up his backside just before he got lost in the press of the herd. The dust was incredible, and we had to wait long seconds for it to settle. Long before we could see anything, we heard his death bellow off in the dust. This dying sound, low, mournful, and unmistakable, is not foolproof, but usually indicates a fatal chest shot. It is an extremely important auditory clue; if you don't hear it, you must approach with extreme caution. I am still cautious even if I do hear it, but this time it was unwarranted. The buffalo was down, finished, less than thirty yards away, but the dust had been so thick we never saw him fall.

It's the Birds

Buffalo have a symbiotic relationship with several kinds of birds, most notably the oxpecker. The buffalo allow the oxpecker, a small, pretty little songbird, to perch on their backs and pick insects. This relationship is strong enough that wherever you see oxpeckers, it's almost certain that buffalo are nearby. Snowy egrets also tend to follow cattle, I believe, to pick through their dung. I have seen egrets circling cattle in the southeastern United States, and you will see the same thing in Africa. If I were a buffalo, I would question any benefits received from the birds, because three times I have had buffalo given away by their feathered friends.

The first time was in Zambia, in 1984. Russ Broom and I had enjoyed a marvelous run of luck, except that the trophy I wanted most, a really nice buffalo, had so far eluded us completely. We left camp in late afternoon to check out an area in our Mumbwa West block that we hadn't yet visited. We drove through Brachystegia woodland cut by numerous open *dambos*, and I assumed we were looking for fresh tracks or buffalo or both. I suppose we probably were, but what we found was egrets, a large number of them whirling over a tree line a few hundred yards away. I didn't have a clue, but Russ knew instantly. "Buffalo," he said flatly, no question.

We headed that way and quickly found the fresh tracks of a good herd, but it was late afternoon, so we followed the birds rather than the tracks. They led us to the buffalo, and there was a good bull in the herd—not a great bull, but considerably better than anything I had taken before. We followed them from one *dambo* to another, seeing the bull several times before we could get a shot. Finally, they held up in one of the openings, and I got a good shot at the bull's shoulder with my .375. He went quite a distance—I can't say why—but he was dead when we found him.

This bull has several tick birds on his back, a relatively common sight. The tick bird and buffalo have a symbiotic relationship, but if hunters are paying attention it's a bad deal for the buffalo. If you see tick birds, buffalo are certain to be nearby. (Photo by Tim Danklef)

I took this buffalo with PH Jasper Samaras in the Selous Reserve in 1994. This was one of the few times in my experience that we never followed tracks at all. Jasper and I were driving along when we saw a moving cloud of red dust, and we maneuvered from there.

The other two instances happened on the same safari in July and August 2004, both with Andrew Dawson and the amazing team he forms with trackers Mukasa and Lummock. The first time, the birds were more a sign of encouragement. The second time, they were pivotal. We were doing the *Boddington on Buffalo* film, and our goal was to take one bull from a herd and a second from a group of *dugga* boys. It was early in the hunt when we left the vehicle just after first light to walk to a hidden spring up in the hills.

At a watering point, you always go carefully, expecting the unexpected. But we were really just looking for tracks, not expecting to find buffalo. It was about an hour's hard walk, and we were a bit more than halfway there, when Mukasa stopped us and pointed upward. Three oxpeckers flew over high (the best trackers, like this guy, are *aware*), making a beeline for the spring. Mukasa and Lummock smiled and nodded. There were buffalo at the spring.

A few minutes later, we heard them snorting and bellowing. Instantly, Mukasa, in the lead, took us away from the trail to better use the wind. A big herd of at least two hundred buffalo were watering and feeding in the marshy runoff below the spring. We were on top of them for most of the morning before I shot a really beautiful bull trailing the herd.

For the next ten days, we got into buffalo every single day—big herds, small herds, bachelor groups, and *dugga* boys. There were lots of buffalo in the area at that time, as many as I've seen anywhere. The valley is thick, so it was almost all pure tracking, but there was rarely a problem finding tracks. We passed up a huge number of beautiful bulls whose bosses weren't quite hard, and we passed up a considerable number of *dugga* boys that didn't quite meet our standards. And then we followed two *dugga* boys away from a small watering hole.

As I've said, it's dicey to follow just two bulls. But Andrew had taken bulls from this watering hole before. The wind was fairly strong and perfect, and his opinion was that they wouldn't go far and that we'd get a look at them in relatively short order. So we followed, and it was one of the most brilliant tracking jobs I've seen. There was much tall, yellow grass, too much, with many yards between clear tracks. And then there was clay soil baked so hard that no impression was left as the bulls meandered slowly and peacefully. We followed for a couple of hours, much of it spent looking for one track at a time, but the wandering tracks and occasional dung showed that we were getting close. The spoor, such as it was, led across a shallow, open ravine and up a very slight ridge.

We started up, and then Mukasa froze and held out a palm. I thought he had seen buffalo ahead, but that didn't make sense because all we could see was a ten-foot rise in front of us. He pointed up, then swirled his fingers down, and then indicated that the buffalo were right over that little ridge. He had seen an oxpecker drop straight down on the far side of that insignificant rise, and there was absolutely no question in his mind: The buffalo were right there.

He dropped back, and Andrew took the lead, me right behind. We crept to the top of the ridge, and I came up beside Andrew, scanning the brushy depression behind. Nothing. Andrew was already indicating that the buffalo were here. Where? Frozen, rifle at high port, I craned my eyes this way and that. I was looking too far. The black spot behind a stout mopane, just twelve yards away, was a bedded buffalo. The black spot to his left, behind a bush just fourteen yards away, was his mate. When they stood, aware of us but uncertain what we were, I shot the larger of the two with the Rigby .470. But for the birds—and Mukasa's uncanny abilities—we would have walked right into them and spooked them, ruining all that wonderful tracking.

Sharing the Herd

When tracking buffalo, it's necessary to pay attention, but it's unhealthy for the focus to be too fixed. There are other things out there in the bush that require attention—sometimes immediately. Honestly, I'm terrified of snakes, but during the

Wherever the two species occur together, buffalo are lions' favorite prey. It isn't uncommon to find human and feline hunters following the same herd. When this happens, it is often wiser to leave the buffalo to the lions, not because of any danger, but because the buffalo herd will be nervous and may well just keep on going.

These days it is almost unthinkable that a lion could be taken without prior arrangements to hunt lion, but as late as 1988, things were different. We were tracking buffalo in Tanzania's Masailand, and so was this lion, so a buffalo hunt quickly turned into a lion hunt.

African winter, when most hunting is conducted, it's rare to see one. You always want to pay attention, but the chance for an encounter is remote. Early in the season, when it's still raining, and late in the season, when it gets hot, well, that's a different story. The snakes are out! The trackers are totally aware at all times, and you need to instantly understand what they're trying to tell you. Just seeing a snake is enough to ruin my day, so fortunately it doesn't happen very often. On the other hand, most of the snakes I have seen have been in the deep bush while tracking buffalo or elephant. I don't worry about it much, but I watch where I'm going!

Far more serious is that elephant often occupy the same bush as buffalo. You're tracking buffalo, but with the wind in your favor, you might well run smack into elephant, and this has happened a whole bunch of times. Usually they will scream and trumpet, scaring the hell out of you and also spooking the buffalo if they are anywhere nearby. Your professional hunter is, of course, fully aware of this, but you need to be equally aware. Elephant bulls

Andrew Dawson and I enjoying my second buffalo in July 2004. This bull and his buddy, two old dugga boys, were bedded just over a little ridge. Had sharp-eyed tracker Mukasa not seen a tick bird homing in, we would almost certainly have spooked them.

will usually go the other way, and fast. Cow herds—which, playing the numbers game, are what you're most likely to encounter inadvertently—are just as likely to charge. While hunting elephant, you can expect to spend a fair amount of time running from cows you've bumped into, but it can happen while you're hunting buffalo, as well. Follow your professional hunter's lead—now, without asking questions!

Not particularly dangerous, but extremely interesting, is the fact that you will often find you are sharing a buffalo track with lions. In most areas where both species occur, buffalo are the lion's favorite prey. In most soils, lions are almost impossible to track, so you may not always be aware of their presence—or you might become aware very suddenly when you hear a low growl or see a tawny form slipping through the brush ahead of you.

Lions are often a key factor in buffalo movement. Unless you're really hard-pressed to find buffalo, the best thing to do if you find lion tracks overlaying buffalo prints is to simply leave the bovines to the lions. For one thing, if you manage to close on them, they will be extremely keyed up and hard to approach. Then again, you might not get that far, for if they become aware the lions are near, they will just keep moving. Therefore, your chances of closing are much reduced to begin with.

In Masailand in 1988, Michel Mantheakis and I were tracking a little herd of buffalo in some very thick riverine cover. It was late afternoon, but the tracks were very fresh, and we had a good chance to close. One of our trackers stopped us, indicating he'd heard something in the brush just ahead and to our left. We stopped, staring into the long grass, and then it came again, a soft, undefined grunt. At least it was undefined to me! Michel mouthed, "Lion."

Remaining dead still, we strained our eyes and our binoculars. When the sound came again, we pinpointed it. There, dimly seen through long, yellow grass, was a nicely maned male lion, lying down, head erect, maybe as close as twenty-five yards. I had a lion on license, and we had some baits out. When he stood, I put the express sights of the .416 Rigby on his shoulder and squeezed the trigger.

The sickening "click" of a misfire was one of the loudest sounds I have ever heard! Michel, assuming I had neglected to load the chamber, glared at me over the sights of his .458. But an unloaded chamber I had not. What I had was a pure misfire, and now I had to get that cartridge out of the chamber and get a new one into it—while the lion stared us down at point-blank range.

I got it done, and shot him just as he started to move. Wisely, due to the thick cover and the proximity, Michel shot just after I did, and a few minutes later we collected a very nice lion, shot twice through the shoulder. Today, with quotas increasingly reduced and prices escalating, it is almost unthinkable that a lion might be taken as a bonus while on a buffalo hunt. But it's just as common as it ever was to suddenly find you're sharing your buffalo hunt with one of the great cats. It's wonderful to see them, and seeing their fresh tracks is almost as good. But when this happens now, I tend to think it's smarter and better to back away and give them first rights.

Charging the Herds
Chapter 8

You don't have to be crazy to hunt buffalo, but sometimes it helps! You also don't have to be in good physical condition. In the Selous, in 2000, my old buddy Chub Eastman, hunting with American professional hunter Marshall Smalling, filled all his buffalo licenses with a hip-to-toe cast on one leg. And not long ago, a wheelchair-bound acquaintance wanted to hunt buffalo. I figured his best odds were in an area with lots of buffalo, so I recommended Luke Samaras, also in the Selous. Heck, he got a great bull with a forty-one-inch spread. On the other hand, being in the best condition possible not only helps, it makes the hunt much more exciting.

If you can handle it, you will probably spend a fair amount of time running after the herds. As I said before, when they're moving, you can move. The wind always matters, but while the herd is running, noise and motion don't matter all that much. There's a good chance they will stop, at least briefly, after a short run, often turning back in formation to face whatever danger might have spooked them. If you can move fast, you have some chance of at least seeing what's there, even if you can't get a shot.

Some professional hunters carry this idea a step further and literally charge into the herd. Nothing is more exciting. Dust and buffalo smell fill your nostrils, sweat runs into your eyes, your heart leaps into your throat, and hoof beats fill your ears. To some extent, this charging in is a desperate move—not desperate because of danger, although there's a little bit of that, but desperate because you are completely giving yourself away (otherwise normally done when a herd spooks and you haven't yet seen what is there). It

Russ Broom and I pose with a really good Zimbabwe bull, about 44 inches wide, taken in the Zambezi Valley in 1992. It was Russ who first introduced me to the technique of "charging the herds" about a decade earlier.

usually doesn't work with bachelor herds, and especially not with *dugga* boys. (They are most likely to keep running all the way to the Sahara!) But with a herd, if you can stay right behind them when they first spook, there is a reasonable chance you can get a good look at them. You might even get a shot.

It could be my lack of experience in northern areas, but it seems to me this charging-the-herd tactic is a technique mostly used by professional hunters from southern Africa. Under certain circumstances, all the several Zimbabwe professional hunters I have been with will charge the herds, and so will the Botswana hunters. It makes sense that this is primarily a southern technique, because down there the heavy bush makes it extremely difficult to sort through the herd. Seeing the bulls is, thus, a huge problem. Desperate though it might be, before you can shoot him, you have to find out if he's there.

Russ Broom introduced me to this technique in Zambia, and I thought he'd gone completely crazy. On the other hand, I was in awfully good shape back then, and I wasn't about to be left behind.

So when the buffalo ran and Russ ran, I ran right behind him. When the buffalo pulled up short in heavy brush and he kept running, I did the same—without having a clue what he was up to. We never saw a good bull that way, but we did cross a couple of herds off our list, as there wasn't anything good in them. Over the next couple of years, Ronnie MacFarlane continued my herd-charging education in Botswana.

Island Hopping

I have never seen the Okavango Delta in full flood, but I can imagine it. The delta itself is not a swamp, but rather a patchwork of flowing channels, palm islands, and papyrus lagoons. Beyond is a low-lying, very flat plain that during the rainy season fills from horizon to horizon, with the few exceptions of more slightly raised areas that become islands. As the waters recede, new grass grows on the plains. The buffalo graze on the plains and find security cover on the "islands" in between, not only the thick, thornbush islands out on the plain, but also the palm islands in the delta itself. You might pick up tracks in the open country, but you can bet they will lead you into the heavy cover.

Following buffalo from island to island is a unique experience. Sometimes you're walking across dead-flat ground where the grass has been burned. Sometimes you're in standing grass. Sometimes you're wading a channel, wondering where the crocodiles are (the buffalo don't seem to worry about this), and the next minute you're into the dense cover of an island, where a face-to-face encounter with a buffalo, a lion, or a mamba might happen at any moment. As Ronnie MacFarlane calmly told me when I asked about snakes, "Well, there's a lot of mamba on these islands." If you really don't want to know, just don't ask!

Buffalo like the thick cover, of course, and when they know they're being followed, they aren't real excited about crossing that dead-open ground to get to the next cover. It seemed to me that Ronnie MacFarlane's buffalo-charging technique was highly developed, although a wee bit mad. Until the buffalo are spooked the first time, everything proceeds as normal, following the

Following buffalo in the Okavango's palm islands is exciting and interesting. You'll get your feet wet, but it's a great buffalo area.

tracks and then working the herds with utmost care, always minding the wind. As we've seen, if you do this long enough, the buffalo will spook. Once they do, the footrace is on, at least for clients that can more or less hold the pace.

I didn't know enough back then to intelligently discuss exactly what we were doing, but it seemed to me the goal was to press the buffalo so that when they reached the security cover of one island or another, they are forced into indecision—which just might make them hesitate long enough for a good look. One day, we actually saw a small group of buffalo retreating into the cover of some thornbush. Ronnie stopped the truck instantly, and we took off. But instead of following the tracks slowly and methodically, which I expected, he took off at a fast trot.

The herd made it through this patch of cover and across a few hundred yards of open ground, just far enough ahead that we could see their tails vanishing into the next patch of cover. Now Ronnie put on the speed. The next opening was smaller, and we could still see their dust when we sprinted to its edge, then circled

Zimbabwe PH Roger Whittall, his hunting team, and I take a break after a tough tracking job. If you're in shape for it, sometimes, under ideal conditions, you can run with a buffalo herd for miles before either you or they tire of the game.

Often, buffalo herds will only run a short distance before bunching and turning to face the danger. You must be in shape to do this, but if you can keep up with the herd (more or less), you can get a good look when they stop— and sometimes you can get a shot.

around. I don't know why Ronnie suspected that the buffalo would hold there, but he did. On the far side, we looked quickly for tracks, found none, and started to move into thick vegetation to look for them. I have no idea where the wind was—I was too out of my own mind to worry about it!

About that time, a buffalo burst from cover to my right and front, headed for open ground over my right shoulder. It was a decent bull, just what I had in mind. I turned and sprinted a few yards on an intercept course, skidded to a stop, and threw up my old Andrews .470. The bull was crossing my front at a slight, quartering-away angle, not very far away, but going very fast. I shot him like a crossing quail, hitting him slightly high in the shoulder where the vertebrae drop down. He folded in midstride and skidded on his nose for twenty feet, raising a huge cloud of dust.

It was perfect, a great moment that I will never forget. But just so you don't think I can shoot like that all the time, under

Zimbabwe PH Andrew Dawson and I stand under a beautiful red mahogany tree in 2004. Dawson is among the many PHs who love to run with the buffalo herds. He and I did this a lot on this safari.

similar circumstances I have missed entire buffalo! The problem with charging the herd is that the shot must be quick, will often be at a moving buffalo, and will almost always be when you're panting for breath. Normal rules apply: If you aren't sure of your shot, don't shoot! Although I have missed buffalo after charging into them and have wounded buffalo under far better conditions when I had no excuse whatsoever, I can honestly say that I have never wounded a buffalo after charging into the herd. I did do something a whole lot worse, though.

Ronnie and I had chased a medium-size herd from one island to another for quite a while, and I suppose we'd run two or three miles in the process, at one point cutting around a long "L" of dry land, while the buffalo took the straight route across through a couple feet of water. When they got on the island, we could see their dust and ran straight toward it. This was a palm island, and a common feature is heavy brush around the perimeter with open ground in the middle. The herd was milling in the open space when we burst through the cover, so we had achieved the indecision that we wanted. They turned to face us in tight formation, and it looked to me like the best bull—he was no monster—was second from right on the right-hand edge.

I have no idea what Ronnie said, but whatever it was, I either didn't get it or I didn't get it right. I pulled off that bull and shot the wrong one just as perfectly as you please. That's another problem when you run with the herds: Any shot you get will be hurried, and in the dust and confusion, it takes a whole lot of experience to pick the right bull—or even the right buffalo—under that kind of pressure. I can do it now, many buffalo later, but I couldn't do it then, and, worse, I didn't know what I didn't know! Again, if you aren't sure, don't shoot. It's a whole lot better to try again than to botch a shot—or shoot the wrong one.

Evening Parade

During the day, charging into the herd is a last-ditch effort to see bulls you haven't seen or split them up enough so that you can get a shot at a big bull you might have glimpsed. In the late afternoon, especially during the last hour of daylight, it's more like a calculated risk. It may not work, but there are factors that make it a lot less desperate.

Buffalo see well at night, well enough that they travel and feed pretty much at will, in total confidence, during hours of darkness. As dusk approaches, they tend to be at their most calm. On the other hand, they know their greatest risk from lions, their only predator, is at night. Herds don't like to split up and don't like to be spread out as darkness approaches, so when spooked in the late afternoon, they tend to run only very short distances before regrouping.

In the late afternoon, time is the real enemy. If you can slip in on them unaware, so much the better, but if the brush is too thick or you can't seem to get the wind right, you have little to lose. No matter what happens, you're going to run out of time, and they will go wherever they're going to go during the night. If you want to get back on them, your starting point in the morning is wherever you left them at sunset. But it's far better to leave them knowing you have seen all the bulls. If there's nothing there, you won't return to that herd. If there is a good one, you might get a shot, and if you don't, you can try again the next day. Over the years, I've spent many afternoons running into buffalo herds with great Zimbabwe hunters like Geoff and Russ Broom, Angie Angelloz, Cuan McGeorge, and Paddy Curtis, and in 2004, Andrew Dawson and I did this several times. After doing it off and on for twenty years, it didn't seem quite so crazy any more. In fact, it seemed to make a lot of sense, and it was darned good exercise in the bargain.

We had one smallish herd that we caught at midday just as they were lying down. As I related earlier, we waited through a few hellish hours of mopane bees until they got up. Then, while they were moving and much more approachable, we cut in and around the herd several times. About an hour before sunset, we finally got ahead of them, and they walked right into us at about ten yards. There was a pretty good bull up front, quite wide and well shaped, but he was still just a bit soft in the center. We passed on him, and, of course, they spooked. By now, Andrew and I were

In camp in the Selous Reserve in 1988 with professional hunter Paddy Curtis. Raised and trained in Zimbabwe, Curtis is another PH who loves to run with the buffalo herds, wherever he hunts them.

Perfect! We ran with the herd and stayed close enough so that we could see them when they stopped to mill. This is one of the most exciting ways to hunt buffalo—and darned good exercise, as well!

pretty well convinced that we had seen them all, but with little daylight remaining, we now had nothing to lose. So when they spooked that last time, we ran with them, staying close behind the herd for more than a kilometer.

When they stopped, we stopped and looked them over, but still nothing. They ran again, but this time, with dusk approaching, they went only a short distance before stopping again. As they stopped, a good bull turned to face us at about forty yards. This is common, especially in the last half-hour before dark. Then the bulls will often come to the edge of the herd to challenge you. Exciting, and you get a good look, but a genuine charge from a bull is still rare. Although a bit winded, I got the rifle up and was ready, but the closer look showed his boss was soft, and I'm pretty sure he was the same bull we'd seen a few minutes before. The other bulls were very young, absolutely nothing in this herd. We turned and headed back to the truck, very pleased and quite certain that we had seen them all.

This kind of thing isn't for everyone, nor is it essential to hunt buffalo effectively. But if you are in good enough shape to run just a couple of kilometers with a heavy rifle, it's one of the most exciting ways to hunt buffalo. Chances for a good shot are slim, but that's OK, because all you're really trying to do is see if the herd holds the kind of buffalo you're looking for. If it does, great, then you know to return to that herd the next day. If you do get a shot, that's a bonus. It's extremely exciting when the bulls stop and turn to face you—as Ruark said, like you owe them money. The likelihood of an actual charge is fairly remote in a herd setting like this, but you need to be ready, regardless. The exceptions are cows with calves, and with these you must be extremely careful. In a herd, cows are more likely to charge than bulls, and if you inadvertently run between a cow and her calf she *will* charge. Immediately.

In this herd, we ran up behind a cow, and she whirled and lowered her head. She was close and she was serious, and we paid attention and stopped. Andrew hissed, "Get ready, she's coming."

Botswana PH Ronnie MacFarlane and I approach—carefully!—a bull that we took by running with the herd. This technique is very common among professional hunters in southern Africa, perhaps because typically thick bush makes it so difficult to sort out the bulls.

Andrew Dawson and I running with a herd just at sunset. Probably concerned about lions, buffalo herds like to remain together just before dark, so they will generally run only short distances before stopping to mill. This is a great way to see the bulls in a herd. (Photo by Tim Danklef)

We were ready, but she didn't do it. After a standoff of a few seconds, she turned and ran off with the rest. On another evening, we had split a herd. Running alongside the largest group, a cow stopped, turned back, and bawled. Oh, but these are the things you watch out for! We stopped instantly, breathed hard, and stood to her. She had left her calf behind, and we heard its answering bawl. She trotted back, found her calf, and they wandered off to another knot of buffalo. We took another deep breath before charging on after the main group.

One morning, we got on a much larger herd in fairly open mopane. It was still early, and they were moving and feeding along nicely. We worked them quite effectively for about an hour, cutting and circling. We saw several bulls, but it was a big herd, and there were many buffalo we hadn't seen. We got ahead of them and thought we had them coming right to us when, at ten o'clock, much too early, they started to lie down right in front of us. Hell! The wind was shifting a bit in our present location, so we withdrew without spooking them and moved around to the rear of the herd. One bull was still up, and he looked pretty good, but there was too much brush to be sure. And then he moved into a dark mass of buffalo and lay down with all the rest. Now, the wind was really getting tricky, so we backed off completely.

And then we did something very intelligent, a thing that I have never done before. We walked away from them, all the way back to the truck (which wasn't all that far away). Then we drove back to camp, had a leisurely brunch and a most enjoyable nap in our nice, bug-proof tents, and at three o'clock, with a steady afternoon breeze, we walked back to where we had left them and maneuvered around to the front of the herd. Our timing was perfect. They were still lying down, but we hadn't waited fifteen minutes before they started to get up again. They moved off at an angle, but the wind was really good, so we got in front of them again and took a perch on a tall ant heap. It was perfect. A knot

Headed back to the truck just at sunset. The very best time of day to run with the herd is the last hour of light, when buffalo don't like to become separated. It's a good feeling when you leave a herd knowing that you have seen all the bulls.

of buffalo with a very good bull among them fed straight toward us. He was a dandy, heavy-bossed with a spread of at least forty-one, possibly an inch or two more. But he was still slightly soft, so we let him walk by and maneuvered some more.

There were a lot of bulls in the herd, and I think we saw most of them. The only really hard-bossed bull we had seen was a heavy-horned old monster, but he was no more than thirty-eight inches wide. Then, as dusk approached, Andrew asked if I was ready. I was, and we charged into the herd. With a really big herd like this, it's spectacular! We had buffalo all around us, snorting and bellowing, and the dust was thick, but they would only trot a few dozen yards, then turn and mill. Several times we had to pull up short, lest we run right into them. A number of bulls turned and faced us at very short range, and each time I snapped up the heavy double rifle, ready. But the right bull just wasn't there. It was right at sundown, and the chase had taken us almost to the road. Perfect. We let them wander off while we enjoyed a red African sunset, and then we turned back to the truck.

What Makes a Trophy Buffalo?
Chapter 9

As far as I'm concerned, when it comes to buffalo, it's the hunt that makes the trophy. If you track him on foot, sort through the herds until you find a mature bull, then make a clean shot, you have a trophy buffalo—and a lifetime's worth of memories. There are two issues here: Hunting him right, and taking a grownup buffalo. Not everyone will agree, nor does anyone have to: These are my personal criteria. So long as it's locally legal, I have no personal issue with taking a buffalo from the vehicle or waiting in ambush at a water hole. For folks unable to walk much or at all, these are perfectly sound options, and a nice buffalo is still a great trophy under such circumstances. However, I strongly believe that those who are physically able to get out and hunt on foot, should. This is because the *experience* is so much superior, so much more, in fact, that I believe it to be far more important than a couple of extra inches of horn.

I also don't have a big problem with the issue of maturity. It's just that over the years I have established my own standards, and full maturity is one of them. As we will see, age doesn't play at all in any record-book measurements, and younger bulls often outscore genuine old *dugga* boys. Buffalo are plentiful, and properly regulated sport hunting has minimal impact on their overall numbers. So, the taking of the occasional younger bull with exceptional horns probably doesn't hurt anything, except that, as is the case with all animals, it seems a shame that a gifted youngster didn't have the opportunity to pass along his genes. So, for me personally, I'm a stickler for taking mature bulls. And so, thankfully, are most experienced professional hunters. But remember, I've been hunting buffalo darn near every year for more than twenty-five years, and the experienced professional hunters I'm

Conformation is pure "beauty points" and means nothing to record-book score—but it means a whole lot when your buffalo is on your wall. By most measurements—boss, width, SCI score—this Selous Reserve bull taken by Art Wheaton is sort of average. But what a beautiful buffalo!

talking about have been hunting them, if not always longer, at least much more intensively than I have. Understanding that record-book measurements do not take into account age, you can establish your own trophy standards. But don't be surprised if your professional hunter throws a fit over the suggestion of taking a bull before his time, even if he has spectacular horns!

If you buy into the concept of taking a fully mature bull, then the defining factor is the boss, the helmetlike base of the horns. A young bull starts out with soft, spongy horn bases sparsely covered with fine hair. As he grows older, these horn bases grow thicker until, in most cases, they are almost completely grown together. A bit of soft hair remains until the bull is perhaps nine or ten years old, but, eventually, the bosses form into solid, hairless horn. It is at this point that we say the bull is fully mature and, thus, shootable. When sorting through the herds, it's usually widespreading horns that first catch the eye. An experienced PH will see this almost instantly, but what he's really looking for is the boss above those horns, which is much harder to see and often requires a very close look.

The boss is just one dimension of trophy quality in a buffalo. To my mind, there are actually three things to consider: Boss width, outside spread, and conformation. You can add a fourth, maturity, which can be *defined* by the boss, at least by eye, but is not the *same* as the boss, since bosses can be very wide before they become fully hard. But in a clinical discussion of trophy size, we can leave maturity out of the mix. The other three are valid, and the first two, boss width and outside spread, self explanatory. The last, conformation, takes a little more thought, because it isn't all "beauty points," since the shape of the horn dictates actual horn length, very important for SCI score.

Let's get into actual record-book criteria right now. Safari Club International takes three measurements on buffalo. They are the overall length and the width of each boss. These are added together for total score. Overall length starts at one horn tip, goes along the outer curve of the horn in the center, angles toward the front of the boss, bridges the gap between the bosses, angles back to the center of the opposite horn, and continues on the outer curve to the horn tip. The bosses are measured at their widest points at right angles to the horn, from where horn meets skull in back to where horn meets skull in front. The current SCI world record, taken in Zambia, in 1998, by Dr. Grady Hogue, measures a truly incredible 141, an amazing bull. The minimum is one hundred, which is actually one of SCI's more difficult minimums to meet.

These days, Safari Club's scoring system is by far the most universal, but the old Rowland Ward system was based purely on outside spread, with a minimum of forty-five inches. This makes for a very wide buffalo and is a difficult minimum to meet. I've taken a couple that would make it, but in a quarter-century of hunting buffalo all over Africa, I have actually seen very few that would go the distance.

I must say that I'm not crazy about either system, although I think SCI's measurement is far superior. If spread is the only criteria, then actual horn length doesn't matter. Nor does the boss. Cow buffalo can grow very wide horns, and, in fact, some of the top-scoring buffalo in the old Rowland Ward book, way up into the fifties in extreme spread, are cows. I don't have anything against harvesting cow buffalo as needed, but I have a bit of

A last-day bull taken in the Selous Reserve. This bull has a nice spread and good conformation, but his boss is just barely hard. Some PHs would call him "mature;" others would not.

trouble with an overdeveloped cow being considered a better trophy than most buffalo bulls that ever lived. Therefore, I think SCI's system is a better representation of what most consider a trophy buffalo. The bosses get full credit, and that's important. But note that spread doesn't figure into SCI measurement at all. Since the largest measurement, by far, will be total length, the key ingredient to a high-scoring SCI measurement is going to be a deep curl and long points. I fully agree with the former, since most of us agree that buffalo horns that drop down below the jaw and curve upward are more beautiful than straight, flat horns that just happen to be wide. Unfortunately, the really long horn tips that score so well by this system are almost always the mark of a fairly young bull. With full maturity, the horn tips start to wear down, so, regrettably, younger bulls with a lot of horn length will often outscore the heavy-horned old bulls that are, at least in my view, the most spectacular trophies.

It's hard to tell from the photo in the book, but my guess is that the current SCI world record was still a fairly young bull. His bosses

Dave Fulson with an incredibly wide-bossed buffalo taken in the Selous Reserve. Bulls with bosses this big are rare, but they immediately stand out in a crowd. These bosses are at least 16 inches wide and possibly as much as eighteen. (Photo by Dave Fulson)

NARROW
34 INCHES

All buffalo bulls are impressive, especially at first, so you need to take a careful look. The outspread ears are probably 32 to a maximum of 34 inches across, so if a bull's horn is as wide as his ears he's narrow, regardless of what else he might have.

are quite good at sixteen inches, but they appear a bit soft in the center, and he clearly hasn't started to wear down his horn tips. But, like I said, it's hard to tell in the photo. It *wasn't* hard to tell that youth was absolutely the case with a big buffalo taken in 1981, at Matetsi, Zimbabwe—but not with Geoff Broom, who owned the concession. This bull had horn tips that curled around like an upside down Marco Polo ram, giving it obvious and impossible length. Geoff knew about the bull, but considered it too young to shoot, so he put out strict instructions that it must be left alone. Irvin Barnhart, a good friend of mine as well as a great and incredibly lucky hunter, was out with one of Geoff's young hunters. Irvin knew what the bull was when he saw it and he shot it. Geoff maintains that he was extremely put out when they came back with this bull, but I suspect he was a lot less unhappy when his area got credit for producing the SCI world record, which that buffalo held for several years.

No measuring system can give credit for everything every hunter wishes it would. It is what it is, and it isn't bad. You can follow it or not, but regardless of score, I still think that boss, spread, and

AVERAGE
37 INCHES

Like it or not, at full maturity, most buffalo bulls have a horn width between 36 and 38 inches, just outside the ear width. A bull like this looks good and is good—and may be superb depending on the bosses and the curl of the horn.

conformation are the three things to look for when evaluating a buffalo. Let's look at each more closely.

Boss

A friend of mine was hunting buffalo in Mozambique, and at that time and place, buffalo were very scarce and very spooky. He and his professional hunter finally got onto a group of some kind, but they were packed in together. The PH kept saying, "Look for the big boss, look for the big boss." Eventually, they spooked with no shots fired, and my friend asked his PH, "How can I tell which one is the 'big boss'?"

We've all had moments like that, but the serious answer to the question is twofold: Use your binocular, and study the base of the horns. Immature bulls may have bosses that appear large, but they also look gray and soft and, in fact, they are. Mature bulls have bosses that look like, and are, solid horn, deeply crenelated and corrugated. They may or may not be grown together, so don't be fooled by that. However, do understand that if the bosses *aren't* close together, then

WIDE
40 INCHES

Unless you put a tape on a bull, you never know for certain. I happen to know that this bull was exactly 40 inches wide. His ears are tattered, and he is also huge in the body, but most of all his horns are clearly well outside his ears.

the bull is probably not very large in that dimension. In extreme old age, a bull may start to shed the outer covering of his horn, so you may start to see white or gray, rather than black horn. The appearance is quite different from the soft, hairy gray of a young bull, and, almost certainly, the horn tips will be heavily worn by this time, so telling the difference shouldn't be difficult.

What is difficult is that like almost any form of antler or horn, individual variance is tremendous. Some bulls grow wide bosses, and others are narrow. A bull with very narrow bosses may have a boss width of just eleven inches, while bosses up to twenty inches are possible. The space between the bosses also varies. The bosses of a really heavy-bossed bull almost meet in the center, but bulls with narrower bosses often have a strip of hairy forehead between. Bulls like this may *never* have the appearance of being fully hard-bossed, even in old age.

If record-book score is important, then you can almost consider the boss as bonus points. Most mature buffalo will have boss widths between about thirteen and fourteen inches, with horn length making up the major difference. Obviously, a boss width in the upper

The ears look small when you see a bull in the mid-40s and beyond. This bull has "flat" horns with relatively little drop, but he's fully mature and for darn sure plenty wide, making him a wonderful trophy.

teens is better—and also extremely impressive—but I have seen very few buffalo (on the hoof, in trophy rooms, in pictures) that have both abnormally wide bosses *and* abnormally long horns.

In terms of judging a buffalo, it's very difficult to get a good enough look to accurately assess the boss width. I tend to class them as "narrow," "medium," and "wide." You don't see a lot of mature bulls that are narrow, but if you see one, you will have to look extra hard to make sure that he really is mature. There will probably be a lot of space between the bosses, and the bosses themselves will not be impressive. Of course, the rest of the horns might be, so you'll have to make the call. Most mature bulls have "medium" bosses in that twelve- to fourteen-inch range, and there is a visual difference between "narrow" and "medium"—the latter sort of *looks* like what a buffalo is supposed to look like, with a helmet-covered skull and horn bases quite close together.

"Wide" is even more distinctive. Your eyes are drawn to the boss immediately, and you say, "Wow!" I tend to like heavy bosses, but if the truth be known, I have never taken a buffalo with really wide bosses. My heaviest-bossed bull had sixteen-inch bosses. You could see them immediately, and there was no question. I mentioned that extremely heavy-bossed bull that gave Andrew Dawson and me the slip in the Zambezi Valley in 2004. His bosses were noticeably bigger, so I'd put him in the eighteen-inch class, which is very rare. There is just one buffalo listed in the current SCI record book that has twenty-inch bosses. This was a Tanzanian buffalo, taken by Bill Backman, in 1993. If you like big bosses, this would have to be the ultimate!

Spread

When speaking about trophy buffalo, most hunters revert to the old Rowland Ward measurement system and talk about spread alone, as in "That's a forty-inch bull." Spread is the most readily visible element of a buffalo trophy and also the easiest to judge. I like spread almost as much as a heavy boss; a really wide buffalo is very impressive. But whether for good or bad, spread doesn't mean all that much to the SCI measuring system. Take the mule deer analogy into consideration: Hunters love to talk about the "thirty-inch buck," but that says nothing about number of points, length of points and beams, or mass. It's much the same with buffalo. A very wide buffalo may have flat horns that come straight out and have little drop. He may have naturally short horn tips, or he may be worn down. Either way, the tip-to-tip measurement that counts so heavily in the record-book score won't be very big.

Personally, I have never cared much about scoring my own trophies for a record book, so I tend to follow the masses and talk about spread. But I realize that speaking only about spread fails to take into account how mature the bull is, how heavy his bosses are, or how long his horns are. Despite the high standards set by Rowland Ward, most hunters reckon a buffalo with a forty-inch spread to be a darned good buffalo. I agree wholeheartedly! And I'd add that most of the time, it's very difficult to find a forty-incher!

Most buffalo bulls at full maturity will be about thirty-six to thirty-eight inches in outside width. A thirty-eight-inch buffalo that has all the rest—well-curved horns and good bosses—is a very fine trophy and, by almost anyone's standards, a better trophy than a buffalo that achieves greater width by growing flat horns that come straight out. So all of these three elements are seductive, but each means little in isolation. Sure, everybody wants a forty-inch buffalo, just like everybody wants a thirty-inch mule deer. I suppose the good news is that a forty-inch buffalo is a whole lot more common than a thirty-inch mulie—but it's still a difficult mark to hit.

Above that magical forty-inch mark, things get increasingly difficult. A buffalo in the mid-forties, assuming he has a little bit of everything else, is a magnificent trophy, and a buffalo in the high forties is the trophy of a lifetime. They do get bigger. I'm pretty sure I saw a buffalo bull in Tanzania that well exceeded fifty inches in width (and he had all the rest to go with it!), but that's the only live buffalo I've ever seen in that class. Still, you hear about them now and again, though truthfully, buffalo this large are rare everywhere. They also certainly are not an East African exclusive. I saw one that had been taken in northern Botswana, back in 1989, and there have been a few taken in Zimbabwe and Zambia. Jack O'Connor's line about "the big ones always look big" applies in spades. If you see a buffalo like that, you will know him—and you'd better shoot him! I had my chance, could have, and didn't. Chances are I will never see his like again, nor will many hunters, ever.

I was in Mto Wa Mbu, with Geoff Broom. We had worked a herd up in the hills most of the day and were just in the process of giving up on them, when we saw three bulls far below us on the opposite side of a steep *korango*. They looked real interesting, even at several hundred yards, so we hustled down our side of the cut and came out almost opposite and slightly above them at maybe a hundred twenty-five yards. It was the simplest thing in the world. The three bulls were behind a thin screen of brush, and then the first bull stepped out, facing us. He took my breath away, not only the widest, but also the biggest and best buffalo I had ever seen.

I was shooting a scoped Dakota .416 Rigby, and it was plenty accurate. I wrapped into a tight sling and put the cross hairs on him. Shooting downhill like I was, I could shoot over his head and into the center of his spine at the top of the shoulder. It was a bit far for a sure thing on buffalo, but a perfectly acceptable shot. Still, I hesitated, confident that in a second or two he would turn broadside and give

Geoff Broom (left) and Jose Bravo found this lion-killed buffalo not far from where we almost got a huge buffalo. Geoff is convinced it's the same animal we let slip away, and even after drying for an unknown time, it's more than 54 inches wide. Few hunters will ever see a buffalo like this. (Photo by Geoff Broom)

me a perfect shot. But he didn't. He took one step, and then another, straight down the bank, disappearing behind some bushes. Oh, Lord, what had we done?

We waited a long time, and he never reappeared. Then the second bull stepped out, and he was the second-largest buffalo I had ever seen. Wisely, I think, Geoff said, "Craig, I don't know where the other one went, but that's an awfully good bull. I think you'd better take him."

So I did. He was forty-seven inches wide and had it all, a wonderful buffalo—but I'm certain the other one was at least six inches wider. Although we hunted hard, I never saw him again—but Geoff Broom might have.

Some time later, not far from there, Geoff found a wonderful old buffalo that had been killed by a lion. After drying in the sun for an unknown period, it was still 54¾ inches wide. Geoff remains convinced it is the same bull we let walk away in the most severe case of hunting hysteria I have ever experienced.

Something that size few hunters would question. Where hunters struggle is in finding that last inch or two between the high thirties and the magic forty-inch mark, and then recognizing it when they see it. There is a pretty good yardstick. A buffalo bull's tip-to-tip ear spread will usually be about thirty-four inches. This is not an exact science; older bulls often have ear tips that are frayed and worn down, and there is also considerable variance in body size. (The difference between fourteen hundred and eighteen hundred pounds is enough to make a difference in everything—both ears and horns!) So, you can't expect perfection, but you can figure a buffalo bull's ear width at a minimum of thirty-two and a maximum of thirty-six inches.

That makes things pretty easy. No matter what the ear width (and no matter what else he has), a buffalo with an outside spread just even with the ears is narrow. He cannot exceed thirty-six inches and is probably a couple inches less. This describes a great many buffalo bulls at full maturity. If the curl is especially deep and the bosses are exceptionally heavy, he may well be a very impressive trophy by anyone's standards, but for darn sure he isn't wide. If he is clearly outside the ears a couple inches on either side (especially if the ear tips look normal), then he is in the upper thirties—no less than thirty-seven, probably thirty-eight, and possibly thirty-nine. In my experience, this describes the majority of buffalo bulls at full maturity, and if you match it with good conformation and a nice, heavy boss, you have a very good bull.

Now, if it looks like he's a solid, genuine four inches outside his ears on both sides, then he is an absolutely certain-sure forty-inch bull, and, depending on ear width, he might be a couple inches wider. This may be the width you're looking for, but you still need to look at the boss. If the boss is hard, I would call such a bull an instant "shooter." If the horns are flat or the tips are worn, he may not score nearly as well as you think he will, but he's still the kind of bull serious buffalo hunters go mad over. The same yardstick applies to bulls that are even wider, but these are so recognizable that you won't take much time at it. If he's way outside his ears, all you need to do is check for maturity and squeeze the trigger.

Jack O'Connor said, "The big ones look big." It remains true with buffalo. If you ever see one that looks like this, don't try to calculate the width or the boss or the curve of the horn. Just shoot him!

Conformation

In chapter three, I noted that the northern subspecies have horns that don't "drop" as much as southern buffalo. Not all southern buffalo have horns that drop; you see some bulls that have horns that come out very flat. But optimally, the horns drop down from the bases, then curve outward and up, with the tips then curling back in and, sometimes, rearward. You want this configuration not only because it is beautiful, but because, if you have any interest in the record book, it's the downward curve and the upward curl that will give you the length measurement.

The rub, of course, is that as buffalo get older, they wear their tips down more quickly than they grow new horn. So, a mature bull is likely to have short, vertical tips that are often thick and blunt, while a younger bull may have several more inches of sharp horn. Older bulls do put more mass in the outer curve of the horn, which I find very attractive, but you won't find that measurement in any record book.

I don't think very many people shoot buffalo based on conformation. Most of us check the spread, then look for hard bosses, and if both are what you're looking for, that bull will have

My best buffalo was taken with Geoff Broom, in 1993, in Masailand's Mto Wa Mbu block—and he wasn't as big as the one that got away. This is the kind of buffalo Tanzania is famous for. They're there, but there aren't a lot of them. Not everyone will see a buffalo like this.

a bad day. Too, unless you can get the buffalo to look straight at you, conformation is the most difficult of the three elements to judge. I don't personally recommend that you get too wrapped up with this one, as the time to accurately assess a buffalo bull is usually very fleeting. Still, it's important to understand that it's the conformation probably most of all that will give you the book score. This is important to many hunters, and if it is to you, then you could be disappointed. Once more: A buffalo bull with horns that drop down nicely and curl around with good, high tips, but which only has a spread of thirty-eight inches, will absolutely outscore a bull with a spread in the low forties and having less drop, less curl, and shorter tips.

Putting It All Together

Very few of my own buffalo have ever been officially measured, and even if they had, I have a "thing" about quoting record-book scores in my own writing. But, just this once, I'll give you a classic example of this. Andrew Dawson and I shot two very nice bulls in 2004. Since we were working on a film on buffalo, we did measure them. The first bull, taken from a big herd, had a spread of thirty-nine inches. His bosses were fully hard and "medium-average" in width. The horns dropped down beautifully and curled around nicely, and the tips were fairly high and sharp. He scored about one hundred fifteen, a score that hardly bumps the world record but is actually quite high. It isn't easy to reach the minimum of one hundred, and very few buffalo bulls will exceed one hundred ten.

The second buffalo was forty inches wide with heavier bosses. He had good conformation, but his horns didn't drop down quite as nicely as the first bull, and his tips were worn. He scored just over the minimum of one hundred, despite greater width and better bosses. This is not only a good illustration of the difference conformation makes, but also age difference. The first bull was a

PH Andrew Dawson and I display our two Zambezi Valley bulls taken in 2004. The herd bull on the left is about 39 inches wide, but its deep hooks and long tips give it a fairly high SCI score. The dugga boy on the right is an honest 40 inches wide and has considerably better bosses, but by SCI's system it measures fully 10 inches less due to worn tips and a more shallow curl. If they were standing side by side, most people would take the one on the right!

herd bull. His bosses were absolutely, completely, fully hard, so he was probably about ten years old. His tips were still high and sharp. He would never get wider, nor would his bosses ever get bigger, but within a year or two, his tips would start to wear and his record-book score would have diminished.

The second bull was a classic *dugga* boy, found in the company of another, very similar bull that was perhaps an inch or two narrower. He was at least twelve years old, more likely fourteen. His horn tips were thick, but had undoubtedly worn down considerably during the previous couple of years.

Both bulls were fully mature. One hit the magical forty-inch mark, one did not. One had better conformation, but the other was clearly older. Which is the superior trophy? I leave that to your judgment, but these are the decisions you may have to make while hunting Cape buffalo.

Where the Big Ones Live
Chapter 10

I don't mean to kick a dead horse, but throughout this volume I have repeatedly said that with buffalo, so long as you're talking about grownup bulls hunted fair and square, the experience is more important than sheer trophy size. I truly believe that, strongly enough that I want to keep emphasizing the point. That said, given a choice, I think we would all like to take the best bull we can find, maybe even especially today, what with shrinking quotas and increasing license and trophy fees. Over the years I've given a whole bunch of seminars and talks on African hunting, and one question that almost always comes up, is, "Where should I go for a really good buffalo?"

Some places are better than others, but I don't think there's a certain particular answer to that question anywhere. Big buffalo don't grow on trees, no more than exceptional specimens of any species. Even in the very best places, you won't find the big ones hiding behind every bush, and you can go to some of the very best places and not find a big one. This has happened to me more than once. My first experience with buffalo hunting was up on Mount Kenya, a historical haunt of really big buffalo. We hunted hard and almost exclusively for buffalo, and we got into them with no problems. But we never saw a big one.

Kenya is long closed, so, in recent years, Tanzania's Masailand has become, and with good reason, one of the best-known producers of exceptional buffalo. When I made my first safari there, in 1988, I went with high expectations of finding one of those East African monsters. On the very first hunting day, my partner, Bill Baker, took quite easily one of the best-looking buffalo

I have ever seen, heavy-bossed, with deep drop and a forty-six-inch spread. As if I hadn't known that already, the area obviously produced good buffalo. Michel Mantheakis and I hunted buffalo at least part of every day, and we were always looking for buffalo even when we weren't actually hunting them. We saw many, including quite a few bulls, but we never saw a bull that even approached the forty-inch mark.

Despite some notable failures, overall I have been extremely lucky with big buffalo. Location matters, but no matter how good the area, time of year matters, too. It's also important to hunt hard and well, and it doesn't hurt to be just a wee bit lucky! With that luck, you might run into a monster right off the bat, as Bill Baker did on that 1988 hunt, and as I did, when I hunted Masailand's Mto Wa Mbu block with Geoff Broom, in 1993. Luck can't be counted on, so if you really want a big buffalo, you need to spend your hunting days concentrating on buffalo hunting. You must also be willing to pass up lesser bulls until you see what you want.

I think you also need one more ingredient: Lots of buffalo to look at, though to be sure, this doesn't always hold true. Somewhere about 1979, when I first hunted Humani Ranch with Roger Whittall, we were hunting just a small, remnant population of buffalo that had survived an intensive culling implemented because of hoof-and-mouth disease. On multiple occasions, we followed the tracks of the same big-footed bull, always walking alone. Every time we lost him in thick riverine growth. In fact, I never actually saw him. A bit later that season, another client did, and, as I recall, he had a forty-eight-inch spread! Come to think of it, on that same hunt, Barrie Duckworth and I baited for a big, cattle-killing lion. We never saw him, either, so after I left, Roger Whittall shot the lion himself. He's still on the wall at Humani, big and black-maned! So luck counts heavily (good and bad), but overall, I'll repeat that I think it's a numbers game. The more buffalo you have to look at, the better your chances of finding a big one. The corollary to that theory is that I honestly believe that every area that has buffalo is capable of producing big buffalo, and if there are lots of buffalo around, there are almost certainly some bulls that have grown to their full potential.

PH Pete Fourie and Delbert Lesser with the best buffalo I have ever seen come out of the Selous Reserve, taken in 2004 in Luke Samaras' blocks. This bull has it all—huge bosses, wide spread, and wonderful conformation.

Botswana is not known for producing big buffalo, and it's true that, on average, Botswana buffalo tend to have heavy bosses but modest spreads. On the other hand, in both the Chobe and the Okavango areas, Botswana has a lot of buffalo, and there are some very big ones. I mentioned that fifty-inch set of horns I saw in camp. Other hunters I know have taken Botswana bulls well into the forties, including a wonderfully wide, heavy-bossed old bull taken while I was there in 1985. As is the case everywhere, it takes a bit of luck and willingness to keep looking until you see a big one.

South Africa is the opposite situation, producing very big buffalo. If you doubt that, take a trip through Kruger Park! However, South Africa has relatively few huntable buffalo, so the numbers don't work in your favor. Even so, genetics count, and among the relatively few buffalo taken annually in South Africa, you will find some very big ones.

Mozambique is a special case. At least historically, the buffalo were incredibly plentiful, and wherever there are lots of buffalo, there will be some big ones. This is especially true along the Kruger Park corridor and in the Zambezi Valley, both definitely "big buffalo areas." Unfortunately, Mozambique's game populations were badly

Average trophy quality in Botswana may be a bit smaller than in countries to the northeast, but there are not only lots of them but also some good ones. Ronnie MacFarlane and Jack Atcheson Jr. pose with the results of a four-hunter, "buffalo and plains game," ten-day hunt. All the buffalo are just fine, and a couple of them are huge.

depleted during the long bush war and are still rebuilding. There is decent buffalo hunting there, but most areas still have remnant populations of incredibly spooky buffalo, so the hunting is difficult. And even though the area can, does, and will produce big buffalo, the numbers game doesn't work in your favor.

I guess the bottom line is that big buffalo are where you find them, and Edition XI of *SCI Record Book of Trophy Animals* (2005) pretty much bears this out. More than twenty-five hundred entries (a *lot* of big buffalo) pretty much come from all over the map. The bulk of the entries come from Tanzania, Zambia, and Zimbabwe, but there are plenty of trophies listed from South Africa, and quite a few from Botswana and Mozambique. There are even three entries from Namibia. Considering that Kenya had been closed for twenty-nine years when that eleventh edition was published, there is a surprising number of buffalo from that country still listed. There is also a scattering of entries from seemingly unlikely places like Rwanda, Angola, and Uganda.

With apologies to those who favor other areas, over the years I have had the best luck with big buffalo in the three countries that dominate these listings: Tanzania, Zambia, and Zimbabwe. Over the last twenty-five years I have made multiple safaris to all three countries. These are where all of my own "big buffalo" have come from, but, in fairness, these are also the countries where I have done most of my buffalo hunting. I have taken several good buffalo from each country over the space of many years, multiple safaris, and with different professional hunters.

As we've seen, what constitutes a "big buffalo" is open to interpretation. I know that I have taken many buffalo with spreads in the high thirties that, should I have measured them, would score higher by SCI standards than some of my "over forty" bulls. But, to keep it simple, I'll stick with the simple outside spread measurement that most of us use when talking about buffalo trophies. All three countries have been good to me. In Tanzania, I've taken a forty-seven, a forty-two, and a couple of forties. Zambia has yielded another forty-seven, a forty-five, and a forty-one. Zimbabwe has given me a forty-four, a forty-two, and a forty. All of us must base things on our own experience, so I do

Wheelchair hunter Hank Donaldson and PH Luke Samaras with a really fine buffalo taken in the Selous Reserve. Donaldson put extra-large tires on his chair and tracked buffalo, taking two really good bulls on his 2004 safari.

not suggest that these are the only places to look for big buffalo, and they may not even be the best. But they are the places that have produced for me and where I will continue to hunt if a good buffalo is one of the primary goals. Let's look at each, taken in purely alphabetical order.

Tanzania

Tanzania, especially Masailand and some areas in the west like the Moyowosi Swamp, is considered *the* place to look for big buffalo today. The record book tends to bear this out. The top ten places, including one tie for fourth, represent eleven buffalo. Four of the eleven were taken in Tanzania. Perhaps of more significance, the top twenty listing, with a couple more ties, represent twenty-four buffalo. Fully half of these, an even dozen, were taken in Tanzania, and there are plenty of Tanzanian heads throughout the book.

I do not question that Tanzania is one of the very best places to look for big buffalo. It is. That Mto Wa Mbu bull I wrote about earlier is my personal best, with beautiful conformation and pretty good bosses in addition to its wonderful spread. Tanzania is one of my favorite places to hunt buffalo, so I don't want to imply that it's overrated. I would say, instead, that it's misunderstood.

Tanzania has lots of buffalo and certainly the genetics within the population to produce really incredible trophies. The hunting conditions are also extremely conducive to good hunting for trophy bulls. The seven- and sixteen-day licenses offer two buffalo, while the twenty-one-day license allows three. In general, the total safari cost in Tanzania is considerably higher than in southern Africa, but once you're in, most of the trophy fees are quite reasonable. Trophy fees for two buffalo in Tanzania are about the same as one buffalo in Zimbabwe. The advantage to Tanzania isn't sheer cost, though, rather it's that you can take a nice buffalo and keep hunting for a bigger one. Mentally, this is a huge advantage, greatly reducing the pressure on both you and your PH.

By the way, this business about Tanzania being an incredibly expensive safari destination isn't universally true. It is if you're talking about lion, leopard, elephant, and the most prized antelope. This book is about buffalo, and operators in Tanzania have far more buffalo on quota than they do the cats and such. Many of them offer shorter buffalo hunts at a considerable bargain. The basic safari costs are probably a bit more than a similar hunt would be in Zimbabwe, but the trophy fees for buffalo and the common game that comes in the package are much less, so it works out to a similar price. Unlike "Zim," you cannot combine the most desirable plains species like kudu and sable (only offered on twenty-one-day license), but if buffalo is the most desired game, these seven- and ten-day Tanzanian buffalo hunts are marvelous.

The other, and far more important, advantage that Tanzania offers is that much of her game country (though hardly all!), is considerably more open than the typically dense woodland of

Paul Roberts and I display our trophies taken on a short hunt in the Selous in 1994 with Luke and Jasper Samaras. Our goal was testing Paul's new .450 Rigby Rimless Magnum, and all of the buffalo we took were very nice bulls.

Any area that has buffalo will have impressive bulls like this. His boss is obviously very good, but does he have the spread to match? The hard part is looking at the entire trophy for enough seconds to be sure. (Photo by Tim Danklef)

Southern Africa that we tend to call thornbush. Mind you, there is plenty of dense bush, from riverine tangles in Masailand to the Selous' amazing thicket lines. But there is also a fair amount of open country. This means that you often catch buffalo in country where you can see them. If you can see them, you can sort the herds, and if you get the wind right, you can probably close for a shot.

It was our first hunting day in the Selous Reserve, and one helluva long day for me. The fog that plagues the central California U.S. coast at certain times of the year delayed my first flight, a little hop from San Luis Obispo to Los Angeles. This messed up everything. I missed my flight to Europe by a few minutes and was in deep trouble. I called Barbara Wollbrink, a great travel agent, and in short order she had me rerouted to Johannesburg, and then up to Dar es Salaam. This is not the most expeditious route, and it started with an umpteen-hour delay in Los Angeles. But I got in to Dar, had a charter waiting, and caught up with the rest of the group just a day late, the morning of the first hunt day.

PH Cliff Walker and hunting partner Art Wheaton met me at a strip on the western side of the Selous. I was nearly dead after three days of getting there. To my absolute horror, they were ready to start hunting—with me! I take my hunting pretty seriously, but not that day. I barely went through the motions, nodding off most of the time and only leaving the truck when I absolutely had to. As I said earlier, on this hunt we were into an incredible concentration of buffalo. And on this first day, I was lucky. We only ran into one herd, followed them for a while, and—thank God—waved off when the wind turned bad.

Finally, it was late afternoon, with sunset—by law, quitting time in the Selous—approaching fast. I had made it, and now I could go back to camp and crash. We came around a bend, and through a thin screen of light brush, a broad, green, wide-open *dambo* stretched before us. In that meadow, like black eight balls on a pool table, was a huge herd of buffalo. I have never been more insistent in my life than when I suggested that Art take the first shot. He had never shot a buffalo. But he was equally insistent that I take the first one "so he could see how it was done." We didn't have a lot of time to argue, so, with genuine reluctance, I let him win.

There was no time for finesse. Using scattered cover, Cliff led us at a fast jog toward the center of the herd. We closed quickly, then duck-walked our way to a big, brush-covered ant heap. Cliff crept around and immediately ducked back and grabbed me. A few seconds later, as I crawled between some trees on the forward surface of the mound, I understood why. The nearest buffalo, all cows, were barely fifty yards away. A little farther out, something just over a hundred yards, a grand bull stood behind a little bush. I wasn't tired anymore! This was probably the most open shooting situation I've ever had on buffalo, so I got reasonably steady, and when he stepped clear and quartered toward me, I shot him very carefully on the point of the shoulder.

The herd exploded and the bull ran with them, but he quickly lagged behind. We ran with them, too, and when he was clear of all the other black bodies, I shot him again, and he went down. Honest, Art, I wish you'd taken that buffalo! He was forty-two inches wide, a very fine bull any time, any place.

It isn't always, or even often, quite that easy, but in Tanzania, you often have a very good chance of seeing what's there. This does not mean there are big buffalo sitting around waiting to be shot. The first time I hunted Masailand, buffalo were fairly scarce. Likewise, when Geoff Broom and I hunted along the Ugalla River, in western Tanzania. There are buffalo in virtually every hunting block in Tanzania, but densities vary within those blocks and, also, with the time of year. As is common in so much of Africa, many of the concessions butt up against her national parks. This was our problem in the Simanjiro region of Masailand; most of the water was in the park, and that's where the buffalo were.

Come to think of it, it was the same in Mto Wa Mbu. Most of the buffalo were to the south at Lake Manyara National Park or up over the top in Ngorongoro Crater. All we had to work with was a few scattered herds that Geoff Broom knew of up in the

This excellent 42-inch bull is my best Selous buffalo, taken on the first hunting day, in 2000, with PH Cliff Walker.

Oh, my, yes! This is what we're all looking for, but very few buffalo like this exist anywhere in Africa. This bull was photographed in Tanzania's Ngorongoro Crater, famous for big buffalo and a sanctuary for more than half a century. (Photo by Geoff Broom)

hills—but we lucked onto three bulls he had never seen before, quite possibly on a walkabout from the Crater.

Up until a few years ago, the Masailand season extended into March, when the country is green from the short rains and buffalo are darn near everywhere. This was a great time to hunt buffalo, but then they shortened the season to match the rest of the country, with the season now from July until December (although much of the country is impassable after the rains begin in early November). This has made buffalo hunting in Masailand much more hit or miss than it used to be. Depending on the rains, you could well find most of the buffalo within the parks and have very tough sledding.

The central part of Tanzania, in and around the great Rungwa Game Reserve, has plenty of buffalo, but the area is not known for really big ones. This probably isn't fair. The Rungwa region is characterized by fairly dense bush, and hunting there is not much different than in the thick bush of Southern Africa. A decade ago, the Moyowosi Swamp, in western Tanzania, produced a tremendous number of big buffalo. Hunting was often quite easy, with buffalo out on the flood plains glassed from afar, then stalked for a shot. There are still good buffalo in the region, and they will come back with better management. But the area was overshot and, at this writing, is nothing like it was. The Maswa region, on the other hand, sort of at the southwestern corner of what we think of as Masailand, has continued to produce exceptionally good buffalo.

For really reliable buffalo hunting in Tanzania, however, my personal favorite spot is the Selous Reserve. It is absolutely true that the Selous rarely produces monsters in the upper forties. I'm not altogether sure why this is, although I'm fairly convinced that Selous buffalo are a bit smaller in the body than most southern buffalo, so horn size may follow naturally. Most Selous buffalo are like buffalo everywhere else, meaning spreads somewhere in the upper thirties at full maturity. But there are lots and lots and lots of buffalo. The Selous is the largest game reserve in the world, about the size of Switzerland, with no villages, no agriculture, and, at least in recent years, virtually no poaching. You will see plenty of buffalo, and if you look at enough buffalo, you will see some that are much better than average.

Earlier, I mentioned the forty-one-inch buffalo my wheelchair-bound friend took. On the same hunt, his partner, also an acquaintance, took a forty-three-inch bull. That's a great buffalo for anywhere and better than any of my own Selous bulls. That forty-two-inch bull I took with Cliff Walker came from the Selous, and I have taken a couple of forty-inch heads there, as well. I have seen a very few that were larger, but couldn't quite get a shot. It took several more days of hard looking, but eventually Cliff Walker found Art Wheaton a bull that was actually a bit better than mine, also forty-two inches, but with heavier bosses.

The Selous Reserve is one of just a couple of areas I've been in when you could reliably say, "Today we're going to get into buffalo." For many of us, this is as important as the possible presence of big buffalo. If you hunt buffalo in the Selous, you

Zambia isn't known for really big buffalo, but Zambia has been good to me, and I have taken some of my best bulls there. This bull, taken in 1984 in the Kafue region, is a massive old monster with a 45-inch spread and very wide bosses.

will see buffalo. It might take some looking to find a really big one, and you might not find a really big one, but you will see plenty of buffalo. Some of Tanzania's other areas do indeed offer somewhat better odds for a big bull if everything is right, but if your timing doesn't match the game movement, you might see very few buffalo.

Zambia

I have done four safaris into Tanzania, and on all four I have taken buffalo, though not in all the areas I hunted. I have also done four safaris into Zambia. As I related earlier, on that first one, in the Luangwa Valley, in May of 1983, I didn't get a buffalo at all. I was successful on buffalo on the other three, all in hunting blocks around the Kafue National Park. In general, I have hunted hard for the buffalo I have taken in Zambia, and I haven't always seen a great many. Still, Zambia has been very good to me, and I have a tremendous fondness for this country.

Zambia has produced my best lion, my best sable, my best sitatunga, my best Livingstone eland, and, of course, she has her rarities like black and Kafue lechwe, Cookson wildebeest, puku, and so forth. She also has very good buffalo. Only one of the top twenty heads in SCI came from Zambia—but remember, it *is* the current world record! Statistically, I've done much better; three of my own ten best buffalo came from Zambia. They were another forty-seven-incher, almost as good as that Tanzanian monster, but with a bit less drop and curl and narrower bosses; that really wonderful, heavy-bossed forty-five-inch bull; and that very nice forty-one-inch head that I think of as my first "good" buffalo. Had we got a shot at him, the wide bull that Russ Broom and I chased one day in Mulobezi would have been high on my list as well.

Although I have rarely seen large numbers of buffalo in Zambia, there is no shortage. It was in the Kafue that Russ Broom and I worked a herd beyond count, at least five hundred and perhaps twice that many. This was in early November, just before the rainy season. As I wrote earlier, we had a tremendous run of luck on that hunt, but it was the very tail end before we saw any buffalo at all. Well, that's not exactly true. We followed a couple of herds until they crossed the boundary into the Kafue National Park, and while driving along the park boundary we actually saw a couple of herds, standing there looking at us on the wrong side of the road. Then, with time growing short, we ran over to Mumbwa West, the egrets led us to a herd, and we shot a very pretty bull.

I was perfectly happy. In fact, elated. With sundown approaching and the cameras in the truck, Russ and I took off at a fast trot to get the truck. We almost bumped into a group of bachelor bulls, and that huge-bossed, forty-five-inch monster was among them. Without hesitation, Russ said, "Shoot that one, now!" Equally without hesitation, I did. That, of course, is a luxury from a bygone day. Today, only in Tanzania, or in quota areas by up-front commitment, could I have taken that second buffalo. That was quite a day!

Although we only had a couple of days more in that area, from that point we were knee-deep in buffalo. I think it was the next

It's important to not get too carried away about size. Any mature buffalo with reasonable spread, hard bosses, and a nice curl is a great trophy. It is also a sensible goal on anyone's first buffalo hunt. This Zimbabwe bull, with a spread of about 37 inches, was Jim Morey's first buffalo. We had a great hunt, and there's nothing at all wrong with this bull.

day, or the day following, that we got into that monstrous herd. Suddenly, there were buffalo everywhere. This is the positive side of a key factor in many Zambian hunting areas in that before we ran out of time, we had plenty of buffalo in our area. Most Zambian hunting blocks are on the periphery of a national park, primarily the Kafue National Park or the two Luangwa National Parks (North and South). There are tons of buffalo in these parks, but the bulk of the population stays there until the water holes dry out, and then they move out into the hunting areas.

This was our problem, in 1983, hunting a Zambia Safaris area between the two Luangwa Parks. This was at the tail end of the great days of Zambia Safaris, and they offered very attractive reduced rates on the shoulders of the season. In my case, in May, it was a bit too early. There was plenty of plains game of all types. I got a lion, and my partner got a lovely leopard. My old friend, "Buffalo Bill" Sims, got a leopard and a buffalo. Bob Tatsch, a great friend who was almost like a second father to me, got *two* buffalo.

But my partner and I never had a chance at one. We followed a couple of herds to the park boundary, and we saw one small group with no bulls. The buffalo were just starting to come in from the park; Sims and Tatsch got theirs late in the hunt, but I was never in the right place at the right time. Later on, those areas are alive with buffalo, but exactly when that happens depends on how wet the year.

The Kafue is much the same, except that the real buffalo movement starts much later. There is plenty of water in most of the Kafue hunting blocks, so there will always be a few *dugga* boys hanging around, but early in the season, most of the buffalo are in the park. I have been there in July, September, and November. In July, all we had to hunt were the few truculent bachelors hanging around the water holes. In September, there were almost no buffalo in our area at the start of the hunt, but a week later the herds began to show up, and everyone took good buffalo. That was 1996. Every year is different, and in 1984, it

Zimbabwe doesn't produce big buffalo? Look at this boy! We photographed this bull on an island in the Zambezi, sort of a "no-man's land" between Zimbabwe and Zambia. It's a small island, so he can't stay there forever. . . . (Photo by Tim Danklef)

was early November before the buffalo showed up in numbers. Obviously, Zambia produces very good buffalo, but in my experience, if buffalo is a key objective, then the later in the season the better.

Zimbabwe

The "word on the street" is that Zimbabwe doesn't produce buffalo trophies as good as Tanzania. I think this is hogwash. Four of the top twenty trophies in the SCI book came from Zimbabwe. To round things out, of the top two-dozen buffalo records, a dozen came from Tanzania, one from Zambia, four from Kenya, two from South Africa, and one from Botswana. This is a pretty strong showing for Zimbabwe's "small" buffalo (and very strong for South Africa, where the harvest is only a fraction of Zimbabwe's).

The difference to me isn't that the buffalo are smaller. Actually, I think they're bigger in the body and often tend to have larger bosses than more northern bulls. The difference is that in Zimbabwe's uniformly dense mopane forest and thornbush, it's very difficult to sort through the herds to determine what is really there. The vast majority of Zimbabwe's buffalo are found on the periphery of the country: The Wankie (now Hwange) Park corridor to the northwest; the extreme southeastern lowveld, much of it along the Gonarezhou National Park; and especially the huge Zambezi Valley to the north. Much of the Wankie region, which includes famous areas such as Matetsi, is a bit more open, but the lowveld is *thick* mopane forest. Most of the Zambezi Valley is the same—except her infamous *jess* thickets are even *thicker*.

Buffalo hunting is difficult here. Actual sightings of buffalo without tracking are much less common than in all other areas I've hunted, and once you close on a herd, it is usually extremely difficult to sort through them and figure out what is really there. All this aside, Zimbabwe has lots of buffalo and produces a lot of good buffalo. This is not only because the buffalo are there, but also because Zimbabwe's quota system is reasonable and is rigidly enforced. As a result of her current political problems, poaching— primarily meat poaching by hungry people—is more prevalent than it ever has been. This is a much greater problem in the interior ranch country than it is on the borders where the buffalo roam, simply because most of these areas remain very remote and, thus, are largely unaffected.

I believe more buffalo live to old age in Zimbabwe than in any other country in Africa. This was born out on my safari with Andrew Dawson in 2004. Our goal was to take one buffalo from a big herd, then one buffalo from a group of *dugga* boys. This is easier said than done. I've been in areas, like Zambia's Kafue region, where there were a few *dugga* boys around—but I've never been in any place other than the Zambezi Valley where the PH could say we were only going to hunt *dugga* boys, then go out and actually find some, almost on command.

The hunting isn't necessarily easy. As we've seen, in the thick cover even a small herd can be very hard to sort—but that's the fun of buffalo hunting. The Zambezi Valley doesn't have quite the concentration of buffalo that you will find in the Selous Reserve when things are right, but it's close and, overall, probably has better trophy quality.

Concentrate and Pass

Regardless of where you hunt, two things are required to have good odds for a really big buffalo. First, you must concentrate on buffalo hunting. Second, you must be willing to pass up lesser bulls until you find what you're looking for. Buffalo hunting is serious work. When you start a track, you have no idea where it will lead you or how long you will be on it. Once you close with the herd, you might stay with them for the rest of the day—and still not see all the bulls. It's perfectly all right to hunt the odd antelope along the way, but serious buffalo hunting does not go well with cat hunting. For cats, you must check the baits daily, which makes it a bit too late to get on tracks. And if you get on a buffalo track early, that might have been the day you should have checked a certain bait, possibly losing a golden opportunity at a lion or leopard. As in all trophy hunting, you must also keep passing until you see what you want, always understanding that you might not find him. This is especially true today, where it's increasingly unlikely (or a lot more expensive), to have more than one buffalo available.

This is all easy for me to say. As you've seen from some of the stories I've related, many of my best buffalo have been taken by chance, sometimes early in a hunt. That's the luck factor that none of us can do anything about. Sometimes it's good, and sometimes it's bad. I've had as many safaris end with no buffalo at all as I have with a good one that came right off the bat. But the buffalo is a wonderful game animal, and he deserves serious, hard hunting. My Zambezi Valley safari in 2004, which was fourteen days with nothing but two buffalo on the agenda, was wonderful.

So was another Zambezi Valley safari with Russ Broom, that one in 1992. On that particular hunt, it's true that I didn't exactly concentrate. I was hunting leopard and buffalo, a bad combination, admittedly, but this is mitigated if you have plenty of time. We did, fully fourteen days for just those two animals. We checked baits daily (sometimes checked by an apprentice

In Zimbabwe, the typically thick thornbush makes sorting the herds very difficult, but "Zim" produces very fine buffalo if you are a bit patient or a bit lucky, and preferably both. This bull has it all: big bosses, good shape, and a 42-inch spread. I took him in Russ Broom's Zambezi Valley area in 1998.

hunter), and we looked for buffalo tracks all the time. We didn't get into buffalo every day, but man, we got into a lot of them. We ran with the herds and we passed up bulls. Once, I hate to admit, I missed a very nice bull of about forty-one inches. We'd been running hard for a long time, pressing the herd, and when they stopped, I shot right over the top of him.

I think it was just as well. It was somewhere near the tenth day, late in the morning after we'd checked our baits, that we found fresh tracks crossing a road high up on one of the big ridges running down from the escarpment. We didn't follow far before finding them lazing in heavy shade.

Some were bedded and some were standing. One bull seemed to have extremely wide horns, but he was tied up among a mess of cows. We maneuvered a bit and got lucky, with the animals not quite ready to bed for the day. The bull stood, and then stood clear. It was about my sensible limit for iron sights with the double, maybe sixty yards, but I was kneeling and reasonably steady. I shot him quartering away, and as the herd ran, Russ and I raced behind them. We caught him on a slight rise, and I shot him twice more, and then we walked up to have our first really good look at him. His bosses weren't spectacular, but he was forty-four inches wide with a good curl—a bull worth waiting for.

A couple of final notes on hunting big buffalo: Have reasonable expectations, and do some homework so you know what you're looking for. I hope this book will help, and there are other very good books and videos. Don't get tied up with numbers. If you've never hunted buffalo before, don't tie your professional hunter's hands (and your own), by saying you want "a forty-inch bull or nothing." Based on boss width and conformation, many bulls in the high thirties are better trophies than many bulls in the low forties, and you can't always find a really big buffalo, no matter how you hunt or where you are. Enjoy the experience, take the best bull you can find . . . and then come back and look for a bigger one.

Making the Shot
Chapter 11

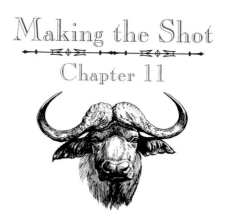

OK, you've tracked the herd and worked them for however long it has taken. You're hot and tired and, admit it, just a wee bit scared. After all, these things are darn near bulletproof, aren't they? There's a good bull, *right there*. You've dreamed about this for a long, long time. Now you must do it. Can you?

Of course you can. Buffalo are extremely strong, and they seem to have overdeveloped adrenal glands that enable them to take an exceptional amount of punishment if the first shot doesn't go right. But it should, and, if it does, you should have no problems. I'm not at all sure you can *hurt* a buffalo, but I'm very sure you can kill him. When it comes time to try to do this, the most important thing is to forget everything you've ever heard, read, or seen about how mean, vindictive, and revengeful he might be. He is no different than any deer or elk you might have shot, and shooting him correctly is really no different. Except for one thing: He is an African buffalo, according to many experts, the most dangerous game of all. You must do it right, but you must also put this innate danger out of your mind and tend to business.

Buffalo *are* dangerous, especially when wounded. There is no question about that. There should also be no question about how strong they are, pound for pound. On the other hand, they are not supernatural, and they are certainly not bulletproof. Much of the stuff written about them is, to be kind, questionable. In Hemingway's *The Short, Happy Life of Francis Macomber*, one of the greatest African stories ever written, Macomber is shooting at a buffalo with his .30-06, and his 220-grain solids are glancing off the buffalo's boss. Maybe, if the angle is just right—but I doubt it.

The wisdom of hunting buffalo with a .30-06 and any bullet is questionable, but I have no question about the capability of any well-constructed bullet—tough softpoints and all solids—to penetrate a buffalo's horn. A decent bullet will cut through it like butter, whether the boss or curve. This is not speculation: I have seen .375 softpoints go right through the heaviest part of a buffalo's horn.

The other thing wrong with this is that Macomber was shooting too high. Maybe he would have stopped the buffalo if the bullet had penetrated, but he really should have been aiming no higher than between the eyes, and probably for the black gun muzzles of the buffalo's nose.

Of course, you don't want it to get to this point. You don't want to have to stop him, which is difficult. You want to kill him, preferably with the first shot. Sometimes this means you must be patient. You don't need a full-on broadside presentation, but you can't take badly angled shots. "Texas heart shots" are out of the question, and anything more than slightly quartering away is almost as bad. The buffalo's paunch is like a fifty-five-gallon drum stuffed with packed grass, and it will soak up bullets like a sponge. Even a solid will not penetrate reliably, and it's unlikely you can get a softpoint through it. You must wait until the buffalo is standing so that you know, *know*, you can get the bullet into his chest.

You must also wait until he's clear of other buffalo. An expanding bullet will probably not exit on a shoulder shot, but if you slip a bit back of the shoulder into the lung area, even a .375 softpoint is likely to go through; larger calibers and solids almost surely will. So, you have to be extremely careful, and it's generally best not to shoot (and definitely not with a broadside shot), if there are other buffalo behind. The head-on presentation offers enough buffalo to stop almost any bullet, but what if you miss? The more clear your bull, the better.

"Clear" also means the bullet's path is clear of obstructions. Forget what you've read about how well the big bullets we use on buffalo will "buck brush." This simply isn't true. Many years ago, when Zimbabwe was still Rhodesia, I got a shot, after a long tracking job, at a buffalo slipping through what was then relatively open mopane.

The three-legged African shooting stick is absolutely wonderful for stability. Janice Fulson is on the stick, husband Dave Fulson is prepared to back her up, and PH Andrew Dawson is calling the shots. (Photo by Dave Fulson)

The buff turned broadside at no more than fifty yards, and I shot very carefully for the shoulder. That was the first buffalo I shot with a .470, and I was really impressed; the animal dropped to the shot and never moved. Now, *this* was a buffalo rifle!

I didn't yet know that body-shot buffalo almost never drop to the shot, no matter what you hit them with. The shoulder was unmarked, but in the neck, almost two feet from where I'd aimed, there was an entrance hole that precisely matched the *profile* of the .475-inch solid I had used. I walked back a few yards and found a very small sapling freshly scarred on one side by a bullet. It was hardly more than a twig and completely unseen over the express sights, but it had been enough to keyhole the bullet so that it hit sideways. It's a wonder I hit the buffalo at all, let alone in a vital spot.

Years later, Paddy Curtis and I tracked up a herd in the Selous, catching them just on the edge of one of those incredible thicket lines that follow almost invisible changes in elevation. I honestly don't recall what kind of bull it was (thus, probably not huge), nor do I recall the shot presentation. I do remember that there was no reaction to the shot, even though I'd been very steady and it felt good. The gun was another .470, though this time I was shooting softpoints. The shot had been about the same distance as that of the long-ago Rhodesian bull, but the branch I hadn't seen was halfway between the buffalo and me. This time I was lucky that I missed him altogether. It happened again in the Selous, in 2000, this time with a scoped .375 Remington Ultra Magnum. That particular hunt was filmed and has aired on television, so there's not much point in denying that it happened. But honest, I really did hit a branch!

The shot needs to be clear, but don't expect your buffalo to be standing in the open. Maybe he will be, but not often! You need to find holes in the branches and leaves to shoot through and you have to match those windows to the spots you need to hit on the buffalo. Sometimes you can shoot through a very light screen of

A big part of getting a good shot means you must wait until the buffalo is clear. Even the most powerful cartridges are very unlikely to plough through obstructing brush. Three times in my career I have shot at buffalo with very adequate rifles only to have unseen sticks or brush send the bullet wild. Twice, fortunately, I missed the entire buffalo. Once, even more fortunately, a bullet aimed at the shoulder hit squarely in the neck, sideways.

grass if the buffalo is standing right behind it, but it doesn't take much to turn any bullet. The farther away from the target, the greater the deflection, and since most buffalo are shot in fairly heavy cover, there will be many potential shots that you can't take. This is frustrating, but you need to wait for the right shot. If you rush it, you might be in for a long, long day!

Shots at Buffalo

Buffalo are very large, and distances of most shots are usually close. Brush and other buffalo are often factors in getting the trigger pulled, and excitement always is. Buffalo get to hunters, and if your hands aren't shaking just a wee bit, you should probably forget this hunting thing and take up something more "challenging." In thornbush, it would be rare to have an opportunity at much past sixty yards, and many shots are a third that distance. In more open country, shooting distances are often greater because there are too many eyes watching to allow a close approach. But a hundred yards is a very long shot on a buffalo, and I can't even imagine a professional hunter allowing a shot at much past a hundred fifty yards.

So, windage and elevation aren't issues, but getting steady and placing the shot are. In Africa, a very common device is the shooting stick. It's made up of three long, slender poles tied together at the top with a strip from an old inner tube. The lead tracker usually carries the poles. He'll set them up when it's time to shoot, and all you need to do is step forward, carefully lay the rifle across them, and take your shot. This is a wonderfully steady system, but it does take some getting used to. I made a set for myself, and I often take them to the range, adding them to my practice regimen.

There are other ways to get steady, such as leaning against a tree or over a branch, but in fast-moving situations at close range, there is often no option but to stand up and shoot. No matter the range, you still have to get steady, so it's important to get in as much shooting practice as you can from actual field positions. When getting ready for your safari, forget about the benchrest. Use it to make sure your rifle is zeroed, and use it again upon arrival in camp

Three-legged shooting stick and a red Cameroon buffalo. In common use throughout Africa, the shooting stick offers a wonderfully steady rest. But, as with any shooting position, a bit of practice is required. You should make your own and take it to the range.

to make sure your rifle has survived the journey. Get away from it between those events, instead spending your time and practice ammo shooting from field positions and over field rests.

Where to Shoot

Buffalo offer a very large target area, but that's not necessarily a good thing. You can't shoot at the whole buffalo, and there's something about a black animal—perhaps because the deer and elk and such that we grew up shooting are brown—that makes visualizing the target area a bit different. Still, even when you get it down to a very precise heart shot, the target area remains plenty big enough. You just have to make sure you understand where the bullet must go and that you can visualize it properly.

Let's start with the broadside presentation. The shoulder/heart shot is the classic shot placement for buffalo and it's pretty hard to beat. The heart lies low, well protected between the heavy shoulders. Follow the centerline of the on leg up into the massive black of the shoulder. The tendency is to shoot a bit too high, but this isn't advisable: Unless you catch the spine, there isn't much up there. In your mind, divide the body into half, horizontally. If you stay away from the upper half, you're in pretty good shape, but if you divide the bottom half horizontally once more and shoot right where that line and the centerline of the on foreleg intersect, you will break one shoulder, make a perfect heart shot, and often break the off-shoulder, as well.

This shot, about a quarter of the way up into the chest, offers the most leeway for errors. A bit low, and you're still in the heart. The lungs lie above and also extend slightly to the rear. The greatest risk with this shot is to shoot too far forward, into the brisket. Chances are, that would be a lost buffalo. There isn't a lot of margin for error, so make sure you are no farther forward than the center of the on foreleg.

A variation of this shot is to use the rear line of the on foreleg and come up anywhere between the horizontal quarter and half lines. In other words, come from one-quarter to one-half up into the chest. This is a central lung shot, just like most of us shoot our deer and elk. The target area is plenty big, the only risk being that you're in big trouble if you shoot just a very few inches too far to the rear.

Neither the heart shot nor the lung shot can be expected to drop a buffalo. The animals are simply too strong and too determined. Most of the time, either shot will send the buffalo off in a bucking canter, and if either shot is truly properly placed, the buffalo should be down within no more than a hundred yards, sometimes much sooner, but rarely longer. Given a choice, I would generally take the central, shoulder-heart shot, but the slightly higher lung shot is useful if the buffalo is standing in grass, a not uncommon situation. The lung shot should be used with a softpoint, never a solid. If it's done right—and this might surprise you—I think buffalo actually go down more quickly than with the pure, classic, heart shot.

Perfect broadside presentations are rare. Usually, the animal is quartering one way or another, and since the distances are usually short and buffalo are quite aware, the facing presentation

Much written about buffalo contains just a wee bit of exaggeration. You don't want to shoot through a buffalo's horn unless you have to, but buffalo are not bulletproof, and the horn won't turn a good bullet. A standard .375 softnose cut through this buffalo horn like butter.

This bull is probably about 125 yards away, a very long shot on buffalo. On the other hand, a dead-steady shot, over a shooting stick and with a scoped rifle, is preferable to a hurried shot at a much closer range. Whatever the shot, you must not shoot until you are absolutely certain of a fatal hit.

also isn't uncommon. Quartering angles are hard to visualize on black animals, and, of course, the steepness of the angle determines where you should shoot. Height on the body, about a quarter of the way up, remains the same. The trick is to visualize the angle and aim correctly. For the last forty years, on all animals, I have aimed for the off foreleg and, on quartering-away shots, tried to angle the shot toward the front of that appendage. On quartering-to shots, the shot is toward the rear of the off foreleg.

This works just fine, but only this year I learned a different and much simpler system from Andrew Dawson. If you can't see the off foreleg at all, then the shot is more or less broadside. If you can see daylight between the forelegs, then you have an angle to adjust for. Dawson's little trick is to simply divide that daylight in half vertically, move up to his horizontal quarter line, and shoot. This will put the bullet more or less into the center of the chest, regardless of the quartering angle.

Frontal shots are exactly the same. Just shoot exactly between the front legs one-quarter of the way up into the chest, and you have a frontal heart shot, very deadly. Typically, the animal will lunge forward several steps at the shot, although very powerful rifles may rock him back on his heels instead. Then he will usually recover and make a death run of a few dozen yards. The quartering-to shot, more or less on the point of the shoulder, is equally deadly and usually will have much the same result. As stated earlier, the quartering-away shot is much trickier. If the angle is slight there's no problem, but it doesn't take much of an angle to place the paunch in the path of the bullet. Elmer Keith called steep, quartering-away angles "raking shots," and if you have enough gun, they're just fine for plains game—but they don't make enough gun for this shot to be sure on buffalo, so a harshly angled shot is the same as a buffalo facing away: No shot at all.

I don't like brain or spine shots at all, at least not on unwounded buffalo. They're tricky, and the target area is small, but they are certainly effective. The brain lies more or less between the eyes, but exactly how to reach the brain with a bullet depends on the angle of the head. In a charge, at least until the last second, the

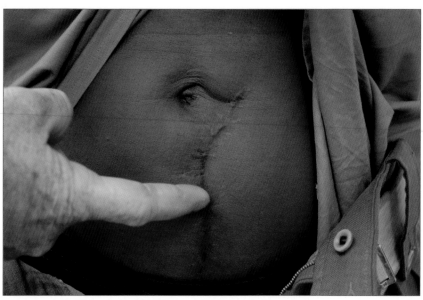

Zimbabwe game scout Wellington Tedzi. If the first shot isn't right, the potential consequences are truly horrible. Wellington, through no fault of his own, was gored so badly that his intestines were lying on the ground. He was incredibly lucky to have survived. (Photo by Tim Danklef)

This is a classic broadside shot on buffalo. The target area is the largest and easiest to visualize. Straight up the centerline of the on foreleg, one-quarter to one-third up the body, and you have a perfect shot.

head is generally up, and you would shoot squarely for the center of the nose, but in a situation where a great bull is in heavy cover and all you can see is the head, concentrate on getting the bullet between the eyes—absolutely no lower, and not much higher, either. Do this only if you simply must shoot. I don't recommend this shot, but if the range is close and you are very steady, it will drop a buffalo in its tracks.

Neck shots, to me, are even trickier, because the neck is huge and it's very difficult to visualize where the spinal column lies. But there is a spine shot that is extremely effective, albeit a bit chancy. The spine drops quite far into the chest between the shoulders. The tendency is to shoot too high, but if you do then all you'll catch are dorsal vertebrae. This might knock the buffalo down, but he'll be up and off in a flash. At the shoulder, the spine is actually fully one-quarter of the way down from the line at the top of the back. A buffalo will drop most spectacularly from a shot placed there, and he will not get up. But I don't recommend this shot. If you miss the spine, you have a wounded buffalo with very little wrong with him on your hands. Most of the time, this shot results from a chest shot

The frontal shot is extremely deadly, ideally placed fairly low in the chest, about one-quarter up from the brisket. Make sure you don't slip to one side or the other, which is the greatest risk here; on buffalo, one lung is just not enough.

incorrectly placed about a foot too high, but I have used this shot on purpose a few times. I do believe this shoulder-spine shot is good to know about, but don't try it unless you are absolutely certain!

Admiring the Shot

My first professional hunter, Kenyan Willem van Dyk, told me that while American hunters tended to shoot fairly well, most had a bad habit of "admiring the shot"—firing the first shot, then waiting to see what happened when they should have been, if not actually shooting again, getting ready to shoot again. More than twenty-five years later, Andrew Dawson used the same phrase, but he was a bit more brutal and didn't single out my countrymen. "Most clients admire the shot, standing around and looking, when they bloody well ought to be shooting."

Dawson was speaking specifically about buffalo, and he's dead right. My personal rule on buffalo is to keep shooting if the buffalo is still on his feet. Why? There are two reasons. First, although calling the shot is an important skill in riflery, it isn't an exact science, and

I like the quartering-to shot. Depending on how steep the angle is, you will probably break the on-shoulder. But you're still after the heart, so keep the shot right around that horizontal line one-fourth up into the body.

nobody is perfect. Even though you think that first shot was perfect, once in a while you will be wrong. Second, even if the shot was perfect, you don't know what the bullet actually did. Today's bullets are better than ever, but bullet failure, though unlikely, is always a possibility. Just keep shooting!

This business of not admiring the shot has been a very hard lesson. I did it on my first buffalo, far up on the slopes of Mount Kenya. He was in a brushy little *korango*, and we were on the hillside above, shooting down. I was shooting a .375 and thought I put the bullet in the right place. I guess I didn't. He took off at the shot, and I failed to shoot again. At first I didn't have a second shot—too much brush. The beginning of the bamboo forest was nearby, and I saw him again as he came out of the brown brush and entered the green tangle. That's when I could have shot again, but I did not. I will never forget the green screen close behind his broad rear end. From the blood—just a drop there and there, and then nothing—I believe I hit him too far forward, through the brisket. We crawled through the bamboo the rest of the day, but I never saw that buffalo again.

Provided the angle isn't very steep, the quartering-away angle offers a very fine shot; your bullet can access the chest cavity without having to penetrate the shoulder first. To find the heart, visually divide the light visible between the forelegs and aim right in the middle.

Admiring the shot has never again been the issue—since Kenya, I have never done that! But I have wounded a few other buffalo (no one shoots perfectly all the time). All have been recovered, several after lengthy, scary follow-ups that might have been avoided if I'd been able to get in a second shot. Sometimes you just can't get a second shot, or your second shot, always hurried, isn't any good. In such cases, you're betting the farm on that first shot. This has happened many times, and mostly you find the buffalo dead. But I prefer to hedge my bets, so I shoot again when I can.

How many shots should it take to put a buffalo down? One well-placed shot will absolutely do it. I have taken a fair number of buffalo with pure, one-shot kills, but these have occurred only under two circumstances: When I was unable to fire a second shot because the buffalo got into brush or other buffalo got in the way too quickly; and when the buffalo dropped to the shot and I could keep my eyes on him, ready to fire again at the slightest movement. Even then, most of these buffalo took a final "insurance" shot during the approach, which I highly recommend.

If the first shot didn't go exactly where you wanted it, then there is no limit to the number of shots it will take. Jack O'Connor wrote a great story about a seemingly invincible buffalo that took fourteen hits from heavy rifles before the episode ended. I haven't seen one take that many, but I have shot buffalo in any combination between one and ten times. No matter how much you might think you want to, you do not want to follow a wounded buffalo (though you certainly don't want to lose a wonderful trophy). Place the first shot as well as you possibly can. Your subsequent shots may not be quite as well placed, but do the best you can and keep shooting.

Upon receiving the first bullet, it is extremely rare for a buffalo to charge, perhaps even more rare than an unprovoked charge. If it happens, it's probably going to happen much later—and you want to do everything you can to prevent it. Most of the time, what happens is that the buffalo kicks it into high gear and heads for cover, usually away from you. Now, I rate a northbound shot at a southbound *unwounded* buffalo as no shot at all, but once you've got that first bullet in him, all bets are off. I'll take that going-away shot as a backup if that's all I have to shoot at (and, incidentally, in recent years, my first shot on buffalo has almost always been a softpoint, but I tend to back it up with solids). Quartering away, you can shoot to break a hip. Going straight away, aim high for the base of the tail. If you hit it, he will drop. If you miss a bit low, a good solid will travel the length of the buffalo, passing above the paunch.

The first buffalo on my 2004 safari appeared out of nowhere. We caught a big herd just as they were leaving a spring, just feeding their way slowly along. Andrew Dawson and I worked our way to the trunk of huge tree at the lower end of a long, narrow meadow. We stood there for two hours, watching buffalo after buffalo parade across the upper end of the meadow at maybe fifty to ninety yards. There were at least two hundred buffalo in that herd, maybe more, and every single one of them crossed the far end of that meadow—except, of course, the best bull in the herd. He came from our right side while we were focused on the major crossing, and I don't think we saw him until he was within thirty yards. One of the trackers hissed, and a second later, Andrew whispered, "Craig, that's a good bull. I think you'd better take him."

A Cape buffalo is not like a deer or a kudu. The buffalo's paunch is like a 55-gallon drum filled with wet grass, and it will quickly stop almost any bullet. If a quartering-away angle is too steep, you simply cannot have confidence your bullet will penetrate. The shot is marginal at this point and is likely to get worse as the buffalo is moving along. Also, shooting any animal on the run tends to result in shots a few inches behind where the placement should be, making a stomach shot all the more likely in this situation.

We had already turned down a dozen bulls and were becoming convinced there was nothing worthwhile in the herd. I had leaned the Dakota .375 against the tree, so I had to grab it, back up so I could see around the tree, and turn hard to the right. The buffalo was within twenty-five yards now, walking slowly toward us, but still partly obscured by brush. "Just wait," Andrew whispered.

Then he stepped clear, facing me, very close, and he looked wonderful. I shot him frontally, and he took the bullet hard and pranced a few steps toward us. This always looks like the beginning of a charge, but almost never is. And it was not this time. He turned to his right, our left, and ran through some thin brush. I shot him again, thought I'd hit a bit far back, and then he came out into the meadow and dashed across the opening quartering slightly away, never more than thirty yards from us. I shot him again as he came into the opening, and again just before he reached the cover on the far side. Both times I saw the bullets hit just behind the shoulder. Total elapsed time was perhaps four seconds.

Dave Fulson got all this on camera, but he was trapped behind the lens, focused on the buffalo. After the buffalo disappeared, he turned to Dawson and asked, "Why did you shoot?"

Andrew grinned. "I didn't."

Were four shots necessary? Almost certainly not—this time. The buffalo went down not ten yards inside the cover, and in seconds, we heard his death bellow. I am convinced the first shot would have done it, although he might have gone a little farther. But that's the way I do it these days, and I think it's a very good habit. One interesting note on this one: The first shot was perfectly placed, and so were the last two as he ran across the meadow. The second shot, fired as he passed through a very light screen of brush, never touched the buffalo at all. That's part of the reason I keep shooting. Rarely is it perfectly clear, and I've lost too many bullets in the brush to ever take a chance again. If I can see the buffalo and he's still moving, I keep shooting.

Forcing the Shot

It's almost as important to know when *not* to shoot as it is to shoot well and often when you have a good chance. Buffalo hunting is extremely hard work, especially in the warmer months, and it's pretty exciting when you finally get up on a herd. It takes steady nerves and discipline, but you simply cannot shoot until you have a good shot—and you must not shoot unless you're sure you've found the bull you want.

It's easy to get a bit desperate after several hours of working a herd, especially as remaining hunting days grow short. It's all right to settle for a lesser bull than you had in mind, especially at the tail end of a safari. It's not all right to mentally commit yourself to a shot before you've even seen the buffalo, but a lot of hunters do this. Always keep an open mind, and be willing to look and walk away. Above all, never shoot unless you fully understand the shot presentation and you're sure you can make the shot.

Now What?

The shots have died away, and so have the hoof beats. What now, Ollie? Most professional hunters stand very quietly for a few minutes, listening. Often you will hear that distinctive death bellow. Hearing it is very good news, and the trackers will immediately smile and offer you the African handclasp in congratulations. Not hearing it is not good news, but also not definitive, because you don't always hear it. Too, sometimes you will hear a crashing in the brush, suggesting that the buffalo has run a short distance, stood, and then gone down.

Sometimes, if the country is open enough, you will run with the buffalo after the first shot, trying to get a second. Usually, you cannot do this, and unless the country is fairly open or the hit exceptionally devastating, you will not see the buffalo go down. Your PH and his trackers are very good at this, and they will have a pretty good idea where the buffalo is hit, provided they were able to see him receive the bullet. But they aren't infallible, any more than you are.

So you wait a little while, and then you start on the track. Most of the time you will find the buffalo down, usually dead. But if you don't find him within a hundred yards, the game changes. Regardless of where you think you hit him, you probably have a wounded buffalo on your hands. So you're going to stop again and regroup, and your professional hunter has some decisions to make. I hope you never have to deal with this, but it's part of the game of hunting buffalo. We'll deal with this phase in a little bit, but next let's turn to buffalo rifles and cartridges.

Bullets, Cartridges, and Rifles
Chapter 12

Many books have been written on the subject of rifles and cartridges for African game, and there are some very good ones. Old John "Pondoro" Taylor's *African Rifles and Cartridges* remains a classic, and I'm told my own *Safari Rifles* isn't too bad. Campfire arguments about which rifle and which cartridge are best will go on forever and are lots of fun, but I don't recommend that you get too wrapped around the axle about any specific choice, whether yours or your buddy's. There are many good rifles out there, and all too many cartridges that are very similar in effect. What matters is that your rifle is mechanically reliable; that you have confidence in it and shoot it well; that your cartridge is adequately powerful; and that your bullet is tough enough to penetrate into the vitals and do its job. This last is very important. Ultimately, it's the bullet that does the work, not the rifle or the cartridge. So I think we will diverge from the normal discussion on this subject and start, rather than finish, with the bullet.

Buffalo Bullets

Not so very long ago, professional hunters were almost universal in recommending nonexpanding, full-metal jacket, "solid" bullets for buffalo. This goes back to the dawn of the smokeless era, when the first primitive, expanding bullets were erratic and unreliable at the then unprecedented velocities enabled by the new propellants. A solid does not expand, but it penetrates deeply. Perhaps the first expanding design that was absolutely reliable for game as large as buffalo was

Checking the sights is an important pre-hunt ritual which allows your PH to check you out while you are checking your rifle. Andrew Dawson uses the VRS system for sighting-in, a wonderfully steady rest.

John Nosler's Partition, invented in 1948. The largest caliber it was ever available in was .375, but this bullet was widely used in Africa, and a few professional hunters came to swear by it. But not all.

When I started hunting Africa, the majority rule was "solids on buffalo," and, indeed, I used solids exclusively until the mid-1980s. By then, expanding bullets had come a long, long way—but they have come much further since then. Note, please, that the bullets you can use depend heavily on the velocity of your cartridge. The higher the velocity, the tougher the bullets you must use. At standard .375 H&H velocity, around 2,530 fps, I simply don't know of any 300-grain .375 bullet that isn't adequate for buffalo; I have used "plain old bullets," like Sierra boattails and Hornady Spire Points, with perfect results. But if you take the velocity up an additional four hundred feet per second to the .378 Weatherby Magnum, you probably want a tougher bullet.

The .416s are the same. At .416 Rigby velocity, 2,400 fps, I've had excellent results with good old Hornady bullets, but up that velocity 10 percent to the .416 Weatherby Magnum, and tougher bullets are called for. Similarly, I have never experienced a bullet problem at the low velocity of the old Nitro Express cartridges. In the days when new ammo wasn't available, I used fifty-year-old Kynoch softpoints with lots of lead exposed, and shot clear through buffalo.

Today, as we know, there are much tougher bullets available. Although they are more expensive, I think most Africa-bound hunters today use them. So do I. Unavailable in large calibers for many years, the Nosler Partition is back in .416, as well as .375. It's a great bullet, as always, but there are several that are even tougher. These generally fall into two categories, the homogenous alloy bullets and the bonded core bullets. The former type is the "expanding solid," either all or mostly copper, with expansion initiated and controlled by a cavity in the nose. The Barnes X, now updated into the Barnes Triple Shock, is the classic, but Winchester's Fail Safe is very similar, differing primarily in that it has a very small lead core in the base. Bullets with bonded cores have conventional jackets and lead cores, but the jacket and the core are chemically bonded together so that jacket and core separation is almost impossible and weight loss is very limited. In African calibers,

Most campfire arguments center on rifles and cartridges, but never forget it's the bullet that does the actual work. I prefer a good softpoint for the first shot on buffalo, with solids for follow-up. These are Woodleigh solids and softs recovered from buffalo—perfect performance.

the most common are Federal's Trophy Bonded Bearclaw; the Woodleigh bullet from Australia; and the Swift A-Frame, which also has a Nosler-like partition in the jacket.

All of these bullets are truly magnificent. Which you should use depends on caliber availability and accuracy in your rifle. I have used all of them, and you can't go wrong with any of them. You still run into a few professional hunters who insist on recommending "solids only" for buffalo, but fewer all the time. Since you must live in the same camp as your PH, and since you don't want to offer him a readily available "I told you so" if you mess up, I recommend following your PH's advice. But he's wrong on the issue of solids, and sooner or later he will come around. Modern softpoints are far more effective for the first shot on buffalo. They penetrate plenty well enough and do much more damage, thereby significantly reducing the follow-up distance.

For the second shot, I'm on the fence. Or, better put, maybe I'm still coming around myself. For many years I have consistently loaded a softpoint up front with solids in the magazine or, in a double, a softpoint in the first barrel and a solid in the second. I still believe

Today there are several really good and really tough expanding bullets that work wonders on buffalo. In addition to the Nosler Partition, Barnes X, and Swift A-Frame, there are the Winchester Fail Safe, Woodleigh, and a few others.

there is validity in this approach. As I mentioned earlier, there's nothing like a solid up the tailpipe to slow a buffalo down. But I am no longer consistent in this approach.

Just a few weeks ago, with Andrew Dawson, I approached those two bulls the oxpecker bird had led us to, with my Rigby .470 loaded with two, 500-grain Swift A-Frames. By the time the bulls shifted around, got clear, and we figured out which was the best, the shot was about twenty-five yards, quartering slightly to me. I hit him with the first barrel, and, of course, he started to run. I swung with him and fired the second barrel, and then I lost him behind a big tree. We heard his death bellow just seconds later, and we found him on the far side of the tree, hardly a dozen yards away. This is about as quick as I have ever seen a heart-shot buffalo go down. Of course, he took a terrible one-two punch; the second bullet landed three inches behind the first, a broadside shot. We recovered both bullets against the hide on the far side, and they were perfect, well mushroomed, with almost total weight retention. This is what modern softpoints are all about.

Cartridges

Since at least some of the favorite buffalo cartridges are available in all action types, I think this should be our next topic. This could be very lengthy, as shooters have long been fascinated with powerful cartridges and we have far more to choose from than we really need. I will make no effort to mention every single one of them, and, indeed, there's no need, because many, like the several old British Nitro Express rounds, from the .450 3¼-inch to the .476 Westley Richards, are virtually identical in power. Remember, there are other books on this subject, and our specific goal here is to discuss what works for buffalo specifically.

Minimums and Maximums: In the old days, a great many buffalo were taken with early military cartridges like the .303 British, 7mm and 8mm Mausers, and the .30-06. Buffalo are no tougher today than they were a century ago, and, certainly, a lot of culling is done today with the 7.62 NATO (.308 Winchester) cartridge. Under ideal conditions, very light cartridges like these will definitely kill buffalo. And, if that's true, then mediums like the .318

Westley Richards (.330 caliber), .333 Jeffery, .350 Rigby Rimless Magnum, and our American .33 calibers will certainly do a good job. I have personally taken buffalo very cleanly with .33 calibers and, with the right bullet, would have no qualms about using a .35 Whelen or my little .350 Remington Magnum.

However, I am emphatically against using any of these cartridges on buffalo, and for two very good reasons. First, calibers less than .375 are illegal for buffalo in most jurisdictions. The .375 H&H was introduced in 1912, and during the last ninety-odd years, most knowledgeable hunters of dangerous game—and most African game departments—have concurred that this cartridge, or its power level, is a sensible minimum for game the size of buffalo. I concur, as well.

As far as I'm concerned, the illegality of lesser cartridges ends the discussion, but there is a second point.

It's one thing to kill a buffalo, and it is not difficult if you have the patience to wait for a good broadside shot. If things go wrong, however, stopping him is an altogether different issue. Back in

A new Winchester M70 Super Grade in .375 H&H. The Model 70 in .375 is truly an American classic, going strong since 1936 and still hard to beat.

Zimbabwe PH Cuan McGeorge with a big-bodied buffalo I took with a single shot from a Dakota M10 in .375 Dakota. You can use the single shots if you wish, and most of the time you will get away with it, but you're asking for, if not trouble, backup from your professional hunter.

Botswana in 1989, we had just returned from the day's hunt when a vehicle rolled up with three local hunters. One of them had been badly gored by a buffalo, his belly ripped open and his bowels exposed. We got a plane in to evacuate him to Maun, and I understand he lived. He had wounded a buffalo with his .30-06 and had been unable to stop it when it charged. No thanks!

Is there such a thing as too much gun? The really big guns, including the .460 Weatherby, .577 Nitro Express, and .600 Nitro Express will, with ideal shot placement, actually knock a buffalo down and keep him down. Lesser cartridges are very unlikely to do this, and even these won't do it all the time. But you don't need this much power to hunt buffalo, to kill buffalo, or to stop buffalo. Also, and perhaps more importantly, you don't need to withstand that much recoil (or haul around that much weight in the case of the largest-caliber double rifles). I am personally really comfortable with cartridges ranging from .375 on up to the .416s, and then on up to the true big bores from .450 to .500. I don't want any more than that. If you can handle them and are able to carry them around, then, no, there really isn't such a thing as too much gun. But very few of us can handle the real cannons, and none of us truly need them.

The 9.3mm (caliber .366): This bullet diameter, though rarely seen in America, is very popular among Europeans. You have to be a bit careful with it. The old 9.3x62mm Mauser was very popular, but it's a fairly slow cartridge, propelling a 286-grain bullet at 2,360 fps, producing 3,500 ft-lbs of energy. Loads vary, but the long, slim, 9.3x74R (the "R" stands for rimmed), chambered in so many continental double rifles, is pretty much ballistically identical. Both, though often used, should be considered marginal and are often illegal for buffalo.

The 9.3x64 Brenneke is a horse of a different color. Producing 2,750 fps with a 286-grain bullet, thus yielding 4,790 ft-lbs of energy, it is absolutely the equal of the .375 H&H, and its fans tend to think it's even better. If the stated minimum is ".375 caliber" or ".375 H&H Magnum" then the 9.3x64 isn't quite legal, but anything said about the .375 H&H applies.

The .375s: For some years after my debacle with a wounded buffalo in Kenya, I was convinced that the .375 H&H wasn't enough gun for buffalo. I was wrong, but it took a long time before I truly accepted that incident was altogether my fault; I just didn't hit that buffalo where I should have. If I had, we'd have gotten him, and if it really was a brisket shot, then I don't think it would have mattered much if I'd hit him with a .600. On buffalo, everything starts with the .375 H&H, and for many of us, all discussion should end right there.

The .375 H&H is plenty of gun, and with the modern softpoints we have available today, it's even more gun than it was back in 1912. The great things about the .375 are not only its adequacy, which should never be disputed, but also its versatility and its shootability. You can use a .375 for everything, and most people can learn to handle this level of recoil. I guess I got over my concerns about the .375, because I have probably taken more buffalo with this caliber than any other, and possibly more than with all the rest combined.

For many years, the .375 H&H stood alone. It's still wonderful, but today it has a lot of competition. That contest probably started in the 1930s, when American wildcatters started blowing out and "improving" its long, tapered case. Roy Weatherby's .375 Weatherby Magnum, introduced in the 1940s and replaced by the .378 Weatherby Magnum in the 1950s, is the

I used a Dakota M76 in .375 H&H on my 2004 safari. While the .375 is adequate for buffalo, its real stock-in-trade is its wonderful versatility. I used it to get a precise shot on a tiny Sharpe grysbok, and then to take a good buffalo with no problems at all.

best known of the various, improved versions of the H&H, increasing velocity by as much as 250 fps. Weatherby's faster .375s, especially the .378, achieved a somewhat deserved reputation for premature bullet expansion, but that was long before we had the great bullets we have today.

Roy's son, Ed Weatherby, resurrected the .375 Weatherby a few years ago, and the big .378 is still out there. Dakota also has its .375 Dakota Magnum. Based on the shortened .404 Jeffery case, it fits into a .30-06-length action, but is about 100 fps faster than the H&H. Remington's .375 Remington Ultra Magnum, a long, fat-cased cartridge, offers about the same velocity as the .375 Weatherby (with a 300-grain bullet at 2,800 fps), and John Lazzeroni has a proprietary .375, the 9.53 (.375) Saturn, even faster than the mighty .378 Weatherby.

I have hunted buffalo with the .375 H&H, the .375 Dakota Magnum, the .375 Weatherby Magnum, and the .375 Remington Ultra Magnum. The .375 H&H is adequate, and the faster .375s are "more adequate." Technically, they are also more versatile, since they shoot somewhat

Left to right: .375 H&H, .375 Dakota, .375 Weatherby Magnum, .375 Remington Ultra Mag, .378 Weatherby Magnum. Buffalo cartridges start with the .375 H&H. It is plenty of gun and easy to shoot, but not overpowering. The faster .375s deliver noticeably more energy, but recoil goes up considerably.

flatter, but in buffalo hunting, this really doesn't apply. What does apply is that they have more energy, and I think they hit noticeably harder as a result. Faster .375s, like the Remington Ultra Magnum and .375 Weatherby, produce about 5,000 ft-lbs of energy, which is about the same as the .416 Rigby and most of the Nitro Express rounds. You can see the difference in impact. Unfortunately, you can also feel it! The cost for that increased performance is considerably more recoil. The .375 Remington Magnum and the .375 Weatherby Magnum are both very hard kickers, and the .378 Weatherby is considered one of the most vicious of all cartridges to shoot. With modern bullets, the effects are wonderful, but relatively few shooters can handle this level of recoil.

The Lower .40s: In 1989 when *Safari Rifles* was published, the .416 revival was just starting. Back then, a .416 was sort of a fashion statement. Today, they are downright popular, and well they should be. Across the full spectrum of African game, the .375 is more versatile, but if you're more concerned about dangerous game than plains game,

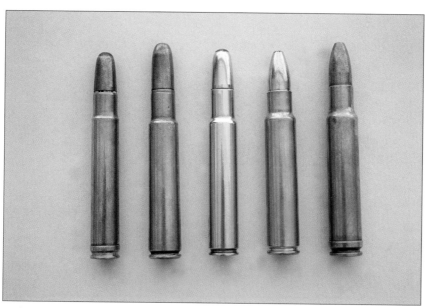

Left to right: .416 Remington Magnum, .416 Rigby, .416 Dakota, .416 Meteor (Lazzeroni), .416 Weatherby Magnum. The .416s (and similar calibers) are not as versatile as the .375, but they deliver considerably more punch on game as large as buffalo. The "slow" .416s, like the Remington and Rigby, are wonderful, with relatively mild recoil. The fast .416s hit considerably harder—at both ends.

then cartridges in the lower .40-calibers are the way to go. Make no mistake, they hit buffalo harder than a .375, they are better able to stop a charge, and they are also far better for elephant hunting.

There are three relatively common bullet diameters in this group. The .416 is far and away the most popular, but let's start the scale with .411. This is the bullet diameter of the two .450-400 double rifle cartridges, the .450-400 3¼-inch, and the three-inch version, also known as the .400 Jeffery. Using a 400-grain bullet at about 2,150 fps and producing about 4,000 ft-lbs of energy, these cartridges are absolutely ideal for buffalo. Historically, they were also the most popular of the large-caliber, Nitro Express cartridges. There are still quite a few .450-400 doubles around, and since they are considered less desirable, are far less expensive than the larger-caliber doubles. I honestly don't understand why the .450-400 hasn't made a comeback. Recoil is comparatively mild, and although the cartridge is a bit marginal

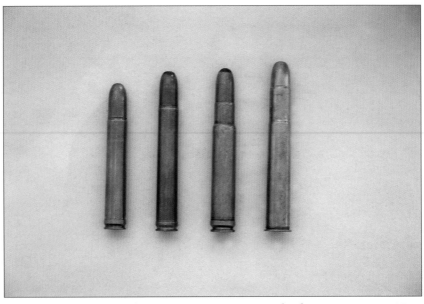

Left to right: .458 Winchester, .458 Lott, .460 Weatherby Magnum, .470 Nitro Express. The true big bores are much more specialized than .375s and .416s. They are clearly better for stopping a charge, but are really useful only for the very largest game. There are many big-bore cartridges, but these four are the most available and most popular today.

for elephant hunting, there's a lot more buffalo hunting than elephant hunting today.

I believe .411 is also the bullet diameter of Holland & Holland's new proprietary .400 H&H, but at this writing, I haven't seen one yet. This was definitely the diameter of the .411 KDF, a short-cased and very effective cartridge that is still seen occasionally, even though KDF has been out of business for some years. Another old-timer that has made a comeback is the .405 Winchester, which also uses the .411 bullet. Be careful with this one. The other .40s made their bones with 400-grain bullets, but the .405 Winchester uses a light-for-caliber 300-grain bullet. It's no pipsqueak, but at the normal 2,200 fps, its light bullet only produces a bit over 3,200 ft-lbs of energy.

Still, Theodore Roosevelt loved it, as did other early African hunters. Larry Potterfield of Midway Arms took his old Winchester 1895 to Tanzania in 2003, where he had no troubles taking Cape buffalo and lion with the .405. Larry showed me his pictures at a convention last year, and I suppose that's what gave me the idea. Ruger now chambers their No. 1 single shot in .405, and I was looking for a low-recoil option for my daughter, Brittany, to use. She tried it, liked it, and, in June 2004, in Australia's Northern Territories, she shot an incredibly huge-bodied water buffalo with the little rifle, killing it cleanly with a single shot. I used it, as well, with equally good results. That said, I'm not sure the little .405 is capable of stopping a charge, so although it would be legal for buffalo in most African countries, I'm not sure it's a better idea than some of the great cartridges of lesser caliber than .375.

The .416 Rigby, introduced in 1911, established a wonderful reputation that actually outstripped its genuine popularity. A proprietary cartridge of the John Rigby Company, relatively few were actually made. But it remained a legend. In the 1970s and '80s, a number of American wildcat (nonstandard) cartridges achieved some level of popularity, most notably the .416 Taylor on the short .458 Winchester Magnum case, and the .416 Hoffman on the .375 H&H case blown out and necked up. The .416 Taylor never quite made it into factory form, but the .416 Hoffman provided the basis for the slightly different .416 Remington Magnum, introduced in 1988. And then there was a small .416 revolution. Within the space of just one year, Remington had their .416, Ruger chambered a magnum version of their bolt action to .416 Rigby (with Federal bringing out a factory load), and Ed Weatherby introduced his belted .416 Weatherby Magnum. All three have become fairly popular. More recently, Krieghoff brought out the rimmed .500-416 for double rifles, and Lazzeroni added the big, fast, 10.57 (.416) Meteor to his lineup.

I have hunted buffalo with the .416 Hoffman (which led to the .416 Remington), .416 Rigby, .416 Weatherby, and .500-416. All are magnificent. The Remington and Rigby propel a 400-grain bullet at 2,400 fps, developing about 5,000 ft-lbs of energy. The .500-416 is just a wee bit slower, while the Weatherby and Lazzeroni are a good deal faster. All are wonderful on buffalo and hit considerably harder than the .375s. But the comparison remains the same: The slower .416s have slightly more recoil than the .375 H&H (though with a bit more gun weight are manageable), while the faster .416s are brutal.

The other, lower .40-caliber bullet diameter that has some popularity is .423. This is the bullet diameter of the .404 Jeffery which, although not nearly as famous, was actually much more popular than the .416 Rigby. Many hundreds of .404s were made by numerous manufacturers, so it's one of those ironic turns of history that this cartridge and bullet diameter are not as popular today as the .416. The .404 Jeffery, although it has a large case, was originally loaded quite mildly. It essentially duplicated in a bolt action what the .450-400 offered in a double: A 400-grain bullet at about 2,150 fps, yielding about 4,000 ft-lbs of energy. The case is large enough to allow considerable hopping-up by hand loading, but the original ballistics make it a very mild and shootable cartridge that is just ducky for buffalo. As is the case with the .416, there were several wildcat .423s, including the .425 Express designed by Whit Collins and my buddy Cameron Hopkins. This one was briefly chambered by Savage, but factory ammo was never made. Then there's the proprietary .404 Dakota, its .423-inch bullet based on a shortened .404 Jeffery case that can fit into a standard-length action. This is a really neat little fireplug of a cartridge that develops a velocity of 2,400 fps and about 5,000 ft-lbs of energy.

So there are plenty of lower .40-caliber cartridges to choose from, and, as you can see, many of them are very, very similar. I will not say they are "better" than any .375. That depends on what you intend to do with them, and also on how much recoil you are comfortable with.

Once you get to Africa, it's much too late to learn how to shoot. A tripod made of sticks is in common use in Africa. A stick tripod is both fast and wonderfully steady, but it takes some getting used to. Make a set at home, and practice with it on your range.

But if I were looking for a cartridge specifically for buffalo hunting, this is the direction I would head.

The Big Bores: I reckon the big bores start at .450 and go on up the scale. Figuring in factory cartridges, proprietaries, and the old Nitro Express rounds, there are dozens. None of them are needed for buffalo hunting. On the other hand, all of them are better for elephant hunting, and if you must stop a charge, bigger is absolutely better. The difference between shooting a buffalo with, say, a .470, and a .416 Rigby is about like the difference between shooting one with a .416 versus a .375. You can see the difference in impact, and the buffalo will usually (though not always), go down more quickly.

Although there are many big-bore cartridges out there, the commonly available choices are the .458 Winchester Magnum; old Jack Lott's .458 Lott, now in factory ammo from Hornady and rifles from Ruger and others; the .460 Weatherby Magnum; and, in double rifles, primarily the .470, although the .500 3-inch Nitro Express has also made quite a comeback. I have personally hunted buffalo with all five of these, and I like them all. As currently loaded by most manufacturers, the .458 Winchester Magnum is a bit slow, rated at (but rarely actually reaching) 2,040 fps for 4,622 ft-lbs of energy. Handloading can bring it back to it original specs of 2,150 fps and 5,000 ft-lbs, but for buffalo, what's the point? Even at the lower velocity, the .458's 500-grain bullet hits buffalo harder than any smaller cartridge. Period. The .458 Lott and the .460 Weatherby are much faster and hit even harder, but recoil goes up fast. There are also a number of other fast, powerful big bores out there, old-timers like the .505 Gibbs and .500 Jeffery, and modern proprietaries like the very similar .450 Dakota Magnum and .450 Rigby Rimless Magnum. All of these are fast, powerful, and hard-hitting—on both ends!

As far as double-rifle cartridges go, there's a long shopping list of virtually identical Nitro Express cartridges: .450 3¼-inch, .500-450, .450 No. 2, .500-465, .470, .475, .475 No. 2, .475 No. 2 Jeffery, and .476 Westley Richards. These cartridges all propel bullets weighing between 480 and 520 grains at velocities from about 2,100 to 2,150 fps, thus all yielding energy in the 5,000 ft-lbs range. All are very effective, but ammo is most

It's really a myth that doubles are inaccurate. Whether or not they are depends largely on the skill and patience of the regulator. This new Rigby double in .450-400 (3") is marvelously accurate, aided by a low-power scope.

available for the .470 which, of course, is a wonderful cartridge for buffalo. The .500 3-inch Nitro Express represents a small step up in power without noticeable additional recoil, so take your pick.

One more big bore deserves mention, because in recent years a number of people have asked me about hunting buffalo with it. That cartridge is the old .45-70, born in 1873 and still going strong. Standard factory loads, with a 405-grain bullet at the original black powder specs of 1,330 fps, are not adequate. However, modern rifles like the Marlin 1895 lever action and the Ruger No. 1 single shot are capable of handling ammo loaded to much higher pressures than the old trapdoor Springfields. With heavy handloads or special factory loads like Garrett's, both featuring bullets of around 400 grains with velocities up in the high teens, the .45-70 will absolutely take buffalo cleanly, and, in recent years, a number of hunters have. I think the situation is about the same as it was when, with full knowledge of its capabilities, I chose to use the .405 Winchester. It will get the job done if everything goes well, but you shouldn't be alone, because I don't think you could reliably stop a charge.

As I've said, there is no reason to consider any cartridges with greater power for buffalo hunting. Big bores between .450 and .500 will do anything that needs to be done on any buffalo, but keep in mind, there is very little versatility. I like to use the big bores on buffalo, but I am not uncomfortable at all carrying a .375. And if I'm carrying a big bore and there is other game on the menu, then a tracker is probably carrying a .375. If you're carrying a .375 or one of the lower .40s, there's really no need to haul a second rifle.

Rifles

Single Shots: We can dispense with this quickly. The single shots are seductively beautiful, and the one-shot concept is marvelous. I have taken buffalo with both the Ruger No. 1 and the Dakota Model 10. I will probably do it again—but I don't recommend it. No matter how good you are, one shot isn't always enough. If you're hunting alone, you're looking for trouble. A friend of Andrew Dawson's was killed in the Sapi area where I hunted while using a single shot. Maybe he would have been anyway, but maybe not.

As for you and me, we probably aren't hunting alone; our PH is there to back us up. But do you really want him to? I don't! While you are fumbling for a new cartridge, he must make a split-second decision as to whether or not he must fire a backup shot. I would prefer to make that decision for him by firing my own backup shots. With practice, you can learn to reload a single shot very quickly, and in relatively open country, you can probably get off a second shot if you need to. But in thick cover, *nobody* is fast enough. For the record, nobody has needed to fire a backup shot on the several buffalo I've taken with single shots. One thing about that one shot is it does make you very careful. But if you mess around with them long enough, you will get into trouble.

Bolt Actions versus Doubles: Both double rifles and bolt actions are available in .375s, lower .40s, and true big bores. The actual cartridges may not be the same, but the available power levels are identical. Between the 1960s and the 1980s, the double rifle had become a rare bird, and the bolt action (primarily in .458 Winchester), was the standard stopping rifle throughout Africa. Today, the double has made a tremendous comeback, both in the hands of hunting clients and professional hunters, so the old, almost-forgotten campfire argument of which is better for dangerous game has new validity.

The bolt action is generally the most accurate, but this doesn't really apply to buffalo; the target is huge and the range should be close. The advantages to the bolt action, then, are its lower cost and its repeat firepower. Cost is an issue if you can't afford something, but I think we should throw that one out. On a purely theoretical basis, does cost really matter if your life is on the line? As for firepower, now you have something. Maybe. A double rifle holds two cartridges, while a large-caliber bolt action holds a minimum of three (with one up the spout), most hold four, and a few hold five. I have emptied bolt actions into buffalo on a few occasions. The question is, did I really need to? Probably not.

Hunters who favor double rifles will tell you that the double handles more quickly and naturally and points better. I think this one is hogwash. Stock fit is stock fit, and I don't see a huge difference, if any, between the handling qualities of a well-fitting bolt action and an equally well-fitting double. The double tends to be a bit heavier, which is a disadvantage, but, lacking a receiver, it is also a great deal

Debra Bradbury (left), Joe Bishop, and Sara Bishop with two good Zimbabwe bulls taken with Barrie Duckworth. Both ladies took their buffalo cleanly with a .375 H&H, always the best combination of adequate power, versatility, and shootability.

shorter with equal barrel length and, thus, more manageable in heavy cover. This is perhaps a slight advantage, but my bolt actions from .375 upwards generally have twenty-four- or even twenty-five-inch barrels, so they are long guns. I have never, ever felt that this was a handicap, not when hunting buffalo, elephant, or even bongo. There is one genuine advantage to the double rifle, however, that cannot be argued away. Nothing else is as fast, or as reliable, for that second shot that just might prevent a long tracking job or, in a charge, save your life.

I'm fast with a bolt action, but there have been several occasions when I couldn't work the bolt fast enough for a second shot. There have been very few occasions when I haven't been able to get off a second shot with a double rifle, and those were all many years ago, before I really learned how to handle and shoot a double. In recent years, never.

This is not to say that the double is better. That instantaneous and totally reliable second shot is a huge advantage, but what matters most is that *you* are comfortable with your choice and that you learn how to shoot it as well, and as fast, as you possibly can.

Scopes versus Open Sights: For more than a hundred years, some hunters have preferred bolt actions, while others preferred doubles.

Both types are perfectly acceptable for all buffalo hunting, so that argument can continue forever. Choice of sights is a more significant debate. Although most double rifles and, perhaps, the majority of big-bore bolt actions wear open sights only, this debate is not about action types. Doubles can perfectly well be mounted with scopes, and bolt actions can perfectly well be left with iron sights only.

Personally, I like to hunt buffalo with iron sights. It adds to the challenge, and it means that I have to get closer. And this statement answers the question. All of us shoot better with scopes, and we can certainly shoot farther and with greater accuracy using scopes. As much as you want to, you can't always get as close as you would like. Had I been carrying an open-sighted rifle, I would not have shot my biggest buffalo at Mto Wa Mbu. This is random, of course, and I have taken other very big buffalo with iron-sighted rifles. But you never know. Skill levels vary widely, too, and the distance at which you can effectively use iron sights shrinks with age. In really good light (which is rare in most hunting), I figure I'm OK at one hundred yards with irons.

Very few times have I removed a scope in favor of open sights. Even so, I believe a dangerous-game rifle should have good open sights and detachable scope mounts. This Weatherby Mark V in .375 Weatherby Magnum has served me well on several safaris.

But all things considered, sixty yards is probably more like it. That might be an average shot on buffalo, but there are many opportunities that are a bit farther. Andrew Dawson and I talked about this, and in his experience as a professional hunter, he figured the use of iron sights probably precluded as much as 60 percent of potential shooting opportunities. That's a big number.

As far as up close and personal and stopping a charge, this depends on the person. I am left-handed and strongly left-eye dominant, so I shoot scopes with both eyes open, keeping my peripheral vision available. Even at very close range I am not handicapped in any way by a low-powered scope. If you are one of those people who must close one eye while shooting with a scope, then the "scout scope" mounted forward on the barrel might provide the answer, as it should allow you to shoot with both eyes open, important at close range.

If you want the biggest buffalo you can find, then a low-powered scope seems almost mandatory. If you prefer the concept of getting in close with iron sights, go for it. Just understand you are reducing the number of opportunities on which you will be able to capitalize. I believe the ideal buffalo rifle, whether double or magazine, should wear a low-powered variable scope, no more powerful than 1.75–6X (and 1.5–4X is just fine). The rifle should also have good, rugged, iron sights. I like a bold gold or ivory bead of 3/32-inch diameter, with a V-notch rear that is so sturdy as to be almost bulletproof. The iron sights should be zeroed, and you should know how to use them. The scope should be set in detachable mounts—that way you can have the best of both worlds. As totally confident as I am with a scope, I usually take it off if I have to go into the thick vegetation after a wounded animal. If things are really close and fast, you may not even use your sights, but instead point the rifle instinctively like a shotgun. In these circumstances, a scope only gets in the way, and what really matters anyway is that the rifle fits you perfectly and handles well. Above all, that's the most important consideration in a buffalo rifle.

The Follow-up
Chapter 13

OK, you spotted a good bull on your edge of the herd. There were too many buffalo to get quite as close as you might have liked (is there such a thing as too close?), and there was a bit of brush. But you got a reasonable shot at a reasonable distance, and you had total confidence in your rifle, cartridge, and bullet. You, your PH, and your tracker are quite sure you hit him well, but he ran with the herd immediately, and only that one shot was fired. Now he's long gone. The dust is still settling, and the mopane forest is suddenly very, very quiet.

Your hands are shaking a bit. And then your palms start to sweat anew as you realize that now you must go into that thick vegetation and find out what you did. Your PH wants to give it a few minutes, so he breaks out a cigarette. You don't smoke, but that seems like a good idea anyway. You replay the shot over and over in your mind. It looked good, it felt good. But the buffalo took more than 4,000 ft-lbs of energy without a shudder, then black bodies erupted everywhere, and he was gone. You haven't heard a death bellow, but the trackers seem confident, still nodding their heads.

Your throat is oddly dry, so you sip some water. Better, but your hands are still sweating. You wipe them on your shorts—again—and your PH stands up, checks the loads in his double rifle, and says quietly, "Let's go see what happened."

You move forward to where your buffalo was last seen. It was a big herd, and there are lots of tracks. How will they ever find which way yours went? All eyes have scanned ahead carefully. There is no sign of any buffalo. You and your PH spread out to cover the trackers as well as you can, and they fan out, zigzagging back and forth, looking for blood, looking for drag marks, looking for the tracks of one bull buffalo that might have departed the herd.

It takes a while, and you replay your shot a dozen more times. Then, a hundred yards along the well-beaten trail of the herd, one of the trackers whistles and points down. All converge, and there's a red splash, bright on the dry yellow grass. "OK, that's him. Good sign. It looks like he left the herd here."

Now the trackers proceed very slowly, scanning ahead. It's too thick to walk abreast, so you're tucked in tight behind your PH, only one tracker ahead of him now. There is blood, but only a few drops and smears. How could you have fluffed such a simple shot? You didn't. You follow for the lifetime of a few more minutes, and then the tracker holds one hand back, palm toward you, and points ahead. You take a step forward, to your professional hunter's right shoulder, and you stare into the brush, seeing nothing. Then, finally, you see a horizontal black line broken by intervening leaves and branches. Your buffalo is down, and he's lying still.

Collaboration

Perhaps things didn't go exactly like that. Maybe there was a bit more brush, and each person—tracker, PH, client—was looking at the buffalo through a slightly different window. You took your shot, and the herd exploded, swallowing your bull. But just as he reached thick cover at the edge of your vision, the seas part, and there's a clear, backside view of your bull. No words are spoken, there isn't time, but you aren't exactly sure which end of which buffalo is yours. Your PH knows you're unsure, but unlike you, he does know which is which, and his big double is up and ready. Should he fire?

No professional hunter worthy of the title will shoot at a client's animal unless he feels it is absolutely necessary. Unfortunately, "absolute necessity" isn't always easy to work out when things are happening fast and there isn't time for discussion about it. The firing of backup shots is probably an issue you and your professional hunter should discuss at the start of the safari. Some clients, especially first-time buffalo hunters with little experience on dangerous game (or, perhaps, gifted with a rare self-knowledge of their own abilities), specifically ask the PH to shoot right after they do on such hunts. Others absolutely insist that no backup shots be fired, no matter what.

I think the first course of action is too extreme, but the latter is downright stupid. Your professional hunter wants you to take your game without his assistance. If this is not his attitude, then you found the wrong man! If he is able to see the shot and the animal's reaction upon receiving the bullet, he will have a very good idea of where the buffalo is hit, and if it looks good, then there is no reason for him to collaborate. On the other hand, he is absolutely responsible for the safety of the entire party—yours, the trackers', and his own. A client's ego is not worth getting someone hurt, so I think it's ridiculous to tie his hands and prevent him from doing his job.

Sure, I would prefer that the PH not shoot, but what that means is that I would prefer to shoot well enough so that he doesn't have to. I leave it this way. At the outset of any safari with a PH I'm not familiar with, I tell him to use his own judgment. In a fast-moving situation, he has to make a split-second decision as to whether or not he should shoot. If he does and I think he shouldn't have, we can talk about it later. Over the years, I've been assisted with a small handful of backup shots on several different potentially dangerous animals and I've never had an issue.

The one buffalo I lost, in Kenya, was lost not only because I made a bad shot, but also because, when he tried to back me up, Willem van Dyk's over/under .458 had a double discharge. I have admitted that I admired the shot, but there's a little more to it than that. I fired, the buffalo ran, and then I heard this incredible sound—like a giant bell—next to my left ear. I looked around when I should have been shooting and witnessed Willem's .458 up in the air, going end over end. Much closer to the ground, Willem was also going end over end, knocked silly by the exponential recoil. God knows where the two bullets went. To this day, I wish I'd placed that first shot better. I also wish his rifle hadn't chosen that moment to misbehave.

The professional hunter, and he alone, must make the decision as to whether or not he should fire. Like all split-second decisions, sometimes he'll be right and sometimes he'll be wrong, but it will be made based on his estimate of what it going on which, in turn, will be based on his experience. Sometimes it doesn't matter. Neither

When you have a good, clear shot, it's wise to shoot him again—even if you're reasonably certain he's dead. This is called "paying the insurance," and for good reasons.

you nor the PH may have an opportunity for a backup shot, so things will proceed as they will based entirely on where your first shot landed. Sometimes, too, the PH misses. He is only slightly more perfect than you are.

In the scenario I laid out above, the professional hunter has a shot. He might tell you to shoot again, but he must keep his eyes on the buffalo. He probably knows intuitively that you have lost track of your buffalo during recoil, but he doesn't know if you're trying to get back on target or if you're standing there waiting to see what happens without having even worked the bolt. He does know that he's looking at the correct buffalo, and just as it vanishes into thick vegetation, he knows he can put a 500-grain solid up its bum.

Should he or shouldn't he? That depends entirely upon what he has seen. He was watching the buffalo very carefully when you fired, and he wasn't interrupted by recoil. If there was no reaction at all, he will probably not fire. While it's possible the buffalo took the bullet in stride, it's more likely that you missed or, worse, shot a different buffalo. Fortunately, most animals, even buffalo, show some reaction upon receiving a heavy bullet. In this case, whether he shoots or not depends upon his interpretation of that reaction. If he believes it was a well-placed killing shot, he will probably not shoot. If he believes otherwise, then I consider it part of his job to get another bullet into the buffalo, placed as well as he possibly can. He is no more infallible than you are, so despite the best intentions, he can't always pull it off. But I'd rather he try than watch the buffalo run off, knowing in his heart that it's very unlikely you'll find it dead.

When He's Down

OK, let's return to our original scenario. The buffalo is lying down, and there is no movement. He's probably dead or dying. Or is he? The old saying in Africa is, "It's the dead ones that get up and kill you." Truer words were never spoken—except that it is ridiculously reckless to be hurt by a downed animal. It happens, but, as I've said, it is almost always a result of serious mistakes. A few years ago, a peer of the realm, the eldest son of the Lord Mountbatten who led the Commandos at Normandy, was killed by a buffalo. As I understand it, this man was an experienced hunter but had never hunted buffalo. After shooting his buffalo and then tracking it for a while, he spied it from a short, but safe, distance. Excited and triumphant, he raced to admire his trophy—and was gored in the femoral artery, dying on the spot.

The lesson here is that no matter how badly or lightly wounded, a buffalo that is lying down cannot hurt you—unless you get within reach of his horns before being absolutely certain all life is gone. The first rule is to approach from the rear, making sure the animal doesn't see you; if the buffalo has enough strength left, eye contact will often trigger a charge. This makes for exciting video footage, but I consider it very foolish, if not downright inhumane and unethical. The whole concept of hunting is to take the animal as cleanly and as quickly as possible. Besides, despite what you might have read, and despite the exciting film clips you've seen, keep this in mind: *Not all charges can be stopped!*

You don't want to play with these odds. It's like the old story about the guy who walked up to the deer and rested his rifle on the antlers. Then the deer came "back to life" and bounded away with the rifle on

Professional hunter Cliff Walker with his prized .577 double. For dangerous game, the PH will always be armed, and you want him to be. My feeling is that it is altogether the professional hunter's call as to when it is necessary for him to use his rifle.

his rack. All you really know is that the buffalo is down. You don't yet know that he's dead, and if he isn't, you don't have any idea how much strength remains. Approach from behind, and then follow the second rule: When you're clear enough, shoot him again.

As I approach from behind, I watch the animal closely. If there's obvious movement or the head is up, I shoot for the spine from behind. I get close enough so that I know I can hit the right spot, but no closer. If there isn't any movement or the head is down, I try to maneuver just a bit so I can put that insurance shot into the spine from a better angle, preferably from behind so I can shoot through the spine and angle the bullet down into the chest area. Brush won't always allow this, so sometimes that insurance shot must be taken from directly behind, into the spine at the base of the tail or, with the buffalo lying on its side, into the chest from the brisket. The basic rules of shot placement still apply: Remember, you're not just shooting *into* the buffalo. At this stage, you don't know if he's dead, so you're firing a carefully placed shot intended to incapacitate or kill him, preferably both.

The reaction from that shot will tell you everything you need to know. If there is no reaction whatsoever, he is probably dead. If there's a lot of movement and struggling, he definitely was not, and you may well need to shoot him yet again. At this stage, everyone is excited and triumphant, and it's easy to be a bit too casual. As with all animals, you can check for eye movement with your rifle muzzle. Do it from as far back as you can, rifle extended with a round in the chamber, safety off, finger on the trigger. Once there is no eye movement, you can relax, unload, and congratulate each other.

Following Wounded Buffalo

Let's change our scenario one more time. The trackers have found blood. You've followed it for a little way, and the spoor is clear, but it leads on into ever-thicker brush. Once you've followed a blood spoor for a hundred yards or so, you must face the reality that you're no longer looking for a buffalo that's down and dead. No, now you're following a wounded buffalo, and he may well be waiting for you somewhere up ahead.

Yes, there's still a chance you will find him dead, but this is no longer what you expect. The spoor may give clues, and if they're there, the trackers will have found them. Frothy lung blood is always a good sign—but with buffalo, one lung isn't enough. Quartering or frontal shots that go too far to one side or the other may feel good and look good, but may result in a long tracking job. Thin, watery blood or dark blood with stomach matter suggests a hit too far back, really bad news. The trackers will quickly find drag marks from a broken leg or shoulder, also bad news.

The trackers are no longer smiling or joking, and your PH's mouth is set in a tight line. They are not afraid; they trust each other, and chances are they have done this many times before. But they are concerned, because very serious business may lie ahead. Your professional hunter now faces another decision. It is absolutely his responsibility to find the animal and bring it to bag. Should you go along? It's your buffalo, so you probably want to. Unfortunately, this one isn't your call. The trackers will go in first, unarmed. More important than finding the buffalo, your PH must protect them. In

Of several dozen, this Botswana bull is possibly the only buffalo I have ever taken with a single bullet and no insurance shot. He was down in open ground and seemed very dead, so instead of firing again we threw sticks—and approached with great care.

your mind, you going along adds another rifle. That's true, but your presence also adds to the PH's responsibilities because he must then try to ensure your safety as well. It also adds to his worries, because when things get sticky, a loaded rifle behind him isn't always a comforting thought.

He must make the decision based on his assessment of your abilities—your shooting, your safe gun handling, and also your physical condition, because this could take a very long time. If you really want to go, you should state that, but you must respect your PH's decision, whichever way it goes. If he says this one is up to him, you must not take it personally. This is part of his job, not yours, and he must think in terms of safety and efficiency. Once more, your ego is not important.

If the decision is that you should go, be ready for a very long day. Drink plenty of water, and pay attention. In open bush, the trackers will proceed only slightly more slowly than usual, but in thick stuff, they will track very slowly, always paying attention. Follow your PH's instructions to the letter. Usually he will want you to stay on one side or the other, rather than behind, so that you have a clear shot with minimal movement. If you are there, and if the circumstances allow, a very good professional hunter will allow you to make the finishing shot. This, of course, is if you see the buffalo standing in cover or slipping along ahead of you. In the case of a charge, all bets are off: It must be stopped. If you get a shot, do the best you can to make it a good one!

Once, in Botswana, we were tracking a buffalo another hunter had wounded. We got into some very thick bush before it opened into a small clearing perhaps fifteen yards across. On the far side, the bush closed up immediately. Right there, almost indiscernible, was a black mass. It looked like shadow, but it was the buffalo, waiting for us. We had been tracking in file because it was so thick, but now we fanned out, the PH on one side, me on the other, and the hunter in the middle. We all put our rifles up . . . and then nothing happened for an interminable time. I simply don't know why the buffalo didn't launch, but it did not. Eventually a rifle went off, opening the ball game, and a couple shots later, the buffalo was down. Later, we learned what had happened. The client, who had sense enough to apologize later, had raised his rifle, then taken it down and put it between his knees while he put in his earplugs. With fifteen yards of open space to work with, I believe we could have stopped the buffalo handily, but good grief!

Understand that every moment on the track of a wounded buffalo is a serious matter. A mistake has already been made, otherwise you would not be tracking a wounded animal. Additional mistakes are not affordable and compound the likelihood of somebody getting badly hurt.

My old friend and mentor, Geoff Broom, who has tremendous experience in this sort of thing, maintains that a wounded buffalo will never stop until he finds appropriately thick cover from which to launch an ambush. This is probably true, but that does not mean that every time you track a wounded buffalo the episode will end in a charge. If you are hunting slowly and carefully, paying attention all the time, it is actually far more likely that you will see the buffalo and end it before he attacks. As I said earlier, around a campfire in Zimbabwe, Andrew Dawson opined that something like just one wounded buffalo in ten will actually charge. He is a careful hunter, so combine that with the incredible skill of his two trackers, Mukasa and Lummock, and I believe this is true—at least in his case. Other PHs, who may be a bit more reckless by nature or aren't so fortunate in their trackers, may have a much higher percentage of charges. But wounding a buffalo should be a rare event, and not finishing it before it has a chance to charge should be rarer yet.

Some buffalo will charge, and some will not. In 1994 in the Selous Reserve, Luke Samaras, Paul Roberts, and I were driving along when four bulls jumped out of some cover and ran up a little rise. All were good bulls, but one was truly exceptional, well into the low forties for spread. I had one more buffalo on license, so we left the car and picked up the tracks. They didn't go all that far, but it was incredibly thick, and we came on them at very close range, just small windows of black buffalo through a green screen. I got on one of them quartering slightly away, but just as I finished the trigger squeeze he started to move. It was one of those slow-motion things where I knew it, but it was too late to call the shot back. I called it perfectly—

Zimbabwe PH Rory Muil and I approach a buffalo, finally down after the scariest tracking job of my career. I shot him badly, hitting him too far back, and we had to leave him the evening before and resume the track in the morning. It was a bad night and a long morning in heavy jess. We finally caught him just as he was turning to charge.

The only way to approach a buffalo is very carefully, from the rear. Avoid allowing the buffalo to see you, and never approach closely until you're absolutely certain he's dead. It's true that "it's the dead ones that get up and kill you"—if you let them.

angling forward from left to right, a little far back, almost certainly through the rear of one lung.

Calling it perfectly didn't make it any better. This buffalo led us through some of the Selous' thickest bush for hours. There were dozens of places where he could have stopped and waited for us—and after several miles of this we were hoping he would, just so we could get it over with. He never stopped at all. When we found him, he was still walking ahead slowly, facing away from us. We finished him there, and he was a very heavy-horned old bull—not the wide one I had hoped for, but a nice old bull. I was shooting a .450 Rigby Rimless Magnum, and the shot, with a 500-grain Woodleigh softpoint, was exactly as I had called it. I can't say for sure, of course, but my guess is, since the buffalo never really stopped, we wouldn't have caught up before dark if I had been carrying a lesser rifle.

I think that was the longest I have ever followed a wounded buffalo. The scariest was in Zimbabwe, in 1998, hunting with Rory Muil in Russ Broom's Songo country south of Lake Kariba. I have mentioned this buffalo earlier. I don't know how I did it, but I made a very bad shot with my .416 Rigby, hitting the buffalo too far back, a pure belly hit. We didn't know this for a long time. I not only shot badly, I also miscalled the shot, so at first I thought we were tracking a dead buffalo.

We hadn't gone much more than a hundred yards, so this was still possible, but then the tracks took us to a sand river that marked the boundary between our area and the Chete safari area. We had to get permission to proceed, which meant a round trip of about five hours to the game guard station. It was very late in the afternoon when we got back on the tracks. We had found only a couple drops of blood, but I was still hoping for a dead buffalo. With little light remaining, we followed into an incredibly thick *jess* tangle on the far side of the river. We jumped the buffalo there, and thank God he didn't charge in that mess! Now we knew what he had on our hands. Watery blood in his bed told the story, a gut-shot buffalo, but it was too late to continue that day.

That was one of the worst nights of my life. I tossed and turned, imaging the buffalo out there hurting and hating. I had seen the *jess* we must follow him in ("*jess*" is the local name for a tangle of heavy thorn peculiar to the Zambezi Valley), and when I awoke, it was bolt upright in a cold sweat, having seen the buffalo coming out of that gray tangle too close to stop.

Russ Broom was in camp, and he loaned me his Rigby double .500, for which I was most grateful. We got on the tracks at six A.M. and followed until late morning. The buffalo had stopped a number of times—in places where we might or might not have been able to see him and stop him. In winter, the *jess* is gray, with visibility measured in feet. When the leaves are on, it is much worse. It was winter-gray now, and our buffalo ambled and circled along slowly, stopping often. In five hours, we covered little more than a mile of straight-line distance, but the track was probably five times that.

Despite my nightmares, it didn't end in a charge, not quite. The wind was turning, and the buffalo was turning with it. We knew we were close, and we were lucky. One of the trackers saw him slipping through the gray thorn ahead, circling to get our wind. I shot him as he turned to charge, then shot him again until he quit moving. With the many sensationalized books and videos out there, I recognize that some hunters go to Africa expecting something like this and feel somehow cheated if things go too smoothly. Trust me, you do not want the situation I've just described. You will follow a wounded buffalo if you have to and if your PH will allow you to come along, but you don't want to put the buffalo through that agony, and you don't want to put your PH and your trackers at this kind of risk.

Here He Comes!

Buffalo do charge, no question about it. The buffalo that killed Bob Fontana came out of nowhere and, as they do, dropped his head at the last and tossed Fontana on his horns. The man turned end-for-end, coming down headfirst. The buffalo met him with his boss, and that was the end. If you have time and space and shoot well and fast, a

Andrew Dawson prepares to fire a backup shot at an outbound buffalo one of his clients has just shot. The client is entitled to an opinion as to whether or not his PH should fire, but ultimately this is the professional hunter's decision, and he must make it instantly. (Photo taken from the DVD *Boddington on Buffalo*)

You never know how long a tracking job will take. You hope it won't be too long, but this is the wrong way to do it on a wounded buffalo. You should not sling your rifle, and you can't let your mind wander. You must be absolutely ready at all times.

buffalo charge can be stopped, but some charges will come so unexpectedly or from such close quarters that they cannot be stopped.

This, then, is a matter not only of luck, but of very careful and very slow hunting. Most professional hunters who have had accidents (and lived to tell about them), concede that they probably went in a bit too fast. The more warning you have and the more space between you and the buffalo, the better the chances of avoiding injury. If you have a bit of distance, even ten yards, you might be able to break a buffalo down or turn him with body shots. But remember that a heart-shot buffalo can travel a hundred yards. Thus, the only reliable way to stop a charge is with a shot to the brain or spine.

Usually, at least until the last second (when it isn't too late to kill him but much too late to stop him), the buffalo will come with his head high. Most professional hunters reckon you shoot for that wet, shiny, double-barrel muzzle of his nose as he comes, sending a solid up through the sinuses, between the eyes, and into the brain. This will surely work, but the target area is very small and he's coming fast. If the angle is available, you might be able to slip the bullet under

"He's going to come!" Are you ready? You must be, and if you can see the buffalo, you must not give him the chance to launch a full-blown charge. The reason for this is that no matter how experienced you are, not all charges can be stopped!

his chin and into the center of his chest. This will surely kill him, but it will stop him only if the shot is high enough so the bullet penetrates back to break the neck.

Geoff Broom, who has stood as many buffalo charges as any man I know (and has never incurred injuries to a client, a tracker, or himself), offers a slightly different perspective. He tries to fade a little bit to one side, then, with the buffalo's head erect, he shoots just under the curve of the horn into the base of the neck. This is a fairly large target area, and if you hit the spine, this shot will absolutely fold a buffalo in midstride. I have never had to try the nasal shot, but I'm sure it works. I have shot a few buffalo with Geoff's "under the horn" shot. It not only works, but is absolutely spectacular.

Whatever shot you choose—or have available—you must make it count. With a double, you might have a second chance, but with a bolt action, it would be rare to get off more than one shot before impact. Wait until the buffalo is clear of brush and you're sure, then do the best you can. One more thing: This business about extra rifles being dangerous is true. Guns are far more deadly than any buffalo that walks. Do not shoot unless you have an absolutely clear shot. In recent years, at least two professional hunters have been shot during animal charges, and if you carry it back, this has happened much too often since professional hunters and clients have been hunting in Africa. The actual seconds during a charge are bad enough, but if a buffalo gets someone down, the risks are even greater. The buffalo must be killed, and quickly, but it isn't a contradiction in terms to say it must be done safely. If your PH is down, it's all up to you, and you have a rare opportunity to be a hero (even though it was probably your fault that the buffalo was wounded in the first place). You must act quickly, but use your head. Place your bullet at an angle so that, should it exit, it can't hurt anyone. Getting shot is the principal fear that drives many professional hunters into taking the track alone. If you are invited, it's a mark of respect. You won't enjoy the experience, but however it ends, you will never forget it.

Cape Buffalo or Water Buffalo?
Chapter 14

To me, it's like fingernails on a blackboard. You've just come back from a great safari, and you're showing pictures to your buddies. Somebody is bound to exclaim something like, "Wow, look at that water buffalo!" As we've seen, not all African buffalo are Cape or southern buffalo, but African buffalo are *not* water buffalo. The water buffalo, long domesticated throughout much of Asia, is just one of several "buffalo," more properly wild oxen, scattered throughout the world.

Unfortunately, the world of wild oxen is shrinking fast. The wild populations of African buffalo are unquestionably the most numerous. Other than a cryptic entry on Appendix One (meaning "endangered"), of CITES (Convention on International Trade in Endangered Species), the status of many of the world's wild oxen is unknown. It is known that the aurochs, the wild ox of Europe, became extinct as much as a thousand years ago. A popular protagonist in the Roman circus, some believe this animal resembled the Spanish fighting bull of today. The American bison, both the plains and wood variety, has made a dramatic comeback from near-extinction, as has the musk ox, now quite numerous in several High Arctic areas. The European bison, or wisent, almost became extinct during World War II, but has recovered somewhat in Poland, and a few other spots. Today, both bison and muskox are readily hunted in North America, as is the wisent on several European preserves, but this hunting is so different from hunting the African buffalo I don't think it adds meaning to our current discussion.

The numerous wild oxen of Asia definitely would. Many of these are found in the true jungles of Southeast Asia, including

Australian PH Bob Penfold looks across a flood plain at several water buffalo bulls. They really do like water and are often seen on marshy plains. They're extremely safe out there; the muck is far too deep to get to them.

Indonesia. Due to their dense habitat, hunting them is more difficult and more dangerous than hunting any African buffalo. Regrettably, this has been a troubled part of the world, with very little game management, and almost no organized hunting programs. Most of these animals are considered endangered, but, in truth, little is known about the current status of most Asian "buffalo" in the wild. The gaur, of course, is the largest of the world's wild oxen, a giant of a jungle beast weighing up to three thousand pounds. Remnant populations exist here and there from India to Southeast Asia, but there is no hunting opportunity. I wish there were. For those of us who love hunting buffalo, this heavy-horned giant ranks as one of the world's great game animals.

Little is known about the status—or even the proper classification—of most of the several wild oxen of Southeast Asia, mystical beasts like the kouprey, mithan, and seladang. Most water buffalo have long since been domesticated, but there is a scattering of wild populations here and there. The water buffalo is not on the Endangered Species list, and there is a fledgling hunting program just getting started in the Philippines. In native Indonesia, the banteng is considered endangered, but it, along with water buffalo, were introduced to what is now Australia's Northern Territories in the middle of the nineteenth century. Both of these wild oxen can be hunted in a free-range status in Australia. There are some other introduced water buffalo populations that can be hunted here and there in places as far removed as South America and South Africa. However, at this writing, in 2004, I believe the only hunting of wild oxen in the world that offers reasonable comparison to African buffalo is that for Australia's water buffalo and banteng.

The water buffalo is by far the most numerous and widespread, once roaming across much of Australia's Top End in tens of thousands. Unrestricted market hunting and helicopter gunning (due to concern about bovine diseases) greatly reduced the population and virtually eliminated water buffalo from most settled areas, but today there are still many thousands of buffalo in Eastern Arnhem Land, mostly aboriginal homelands on the eastern side of the Northern Territories.

The banteng, a small, colorful, wild ox with a reputation for ill temper, was introduced onto the Cobourg Peninsula, northeast of Darwin, as early as the 1830s. Cobourg is a lush, tropical area much like the jungles the banteng calls home. They have thrived there, but the population never expanded significantly onto the mainland and, in recent years, has been contained by a fence across the peninsula.

There are also some water buffalo on Cobourg, but they were apparently of different stock. The animals are smaller in body and generally much smaller in the horn than the water buffalo of Eastern Arnhem Land. There you can still find the legendary "sweepers," with horns spreading several feet across. This is a great hunt, similar to Africa in some ways, but much different in others.

I don't have the experience with water buffalo that I do with African buffalo, but I have hunted these animals several times now, all under the direction of my old friend Bob Penfold's Hunt

A young water buffalo challenges me. I don't think water buffalo are quite as aggressive as African buffalo, but they can and do charge under similar circumstances. This one didn't, I'm happy to report.

Australia Pty. Ltd. The first time was about 1994, when I believe the buffalo population was at its nadir. Helicopter gunning had just concluded, as the practice was becoming too costly and samplings from remnant populations were turning up disease free. Market hunting, primarily for pet food, was also just about over. The survivors had been pushed so deep into the Outback, that it was no longer logistically feasible (or profitable) to recover the meat.

Into the Outback

In many ways, it was a trip from hell. On the map, Australia is just an island, and her Northern Territories occupy only a small portion of it. The Outback is indescribably huge, and I had no idea what I was getting into. Penfold was busy culling donkeys over near Western Australia, so he turned me over to Steve Fullerton and Dave Leonard. Steve, now running his own outfit, is an experienced Australian hunter. Dave is an Alaskan Master Guide, and I've hunted with him several times up there. His wife, Sue, is

Australian, and they spend part of their year Down Under. We started from Steve's house near Katherine, itself a hard, five-hour drive from Darwin. Honest, it didn't look that far on the map!

After picking up some groceries, we left Katherine in the late morning. By dark we were on gravel roads somewhere in aboriginal lands, heading northeast. I think we left any marked roads shortly after midnight, and from then on progress was slow as we winched our way through one bog after another. Jet-lagged from the long trip, I lost it altogether some time after three, and the next thing I remember is pulling into a comfortable tent camp in the gray dawn.

Over the next few days, we saw quite a number of buffalo. I was struck by the notable differences between these and African buffalo, and these differences have held up well on subsequent trips. Asian water buffalo are definitely larger than any African buffalo. I reckon mature bulls start where Cape buffalo leave off, perhaps around eighteen hundred pounds, and a really big bull will easily weigh more than a ton. Also black or charcoal gray in

A typical camp in the remote reaches of Eastern Arnhem Land, the last remaining stronghold of Australia's water buffalo. Other than American-style tents, there isn't much difference between this and a remote African camp.

color, they are blockier in build, with a shorter, wider face and thicker, shorter legs.

I never saw the Outback when there were tens of thousands of buffalo roaming the flood plains, but it's clear to me that water buffalo tend to run in family groups, rather than large herds. I have never seen a herd of more than twenty-odd animals, and even this seems rare. More often you find them in groups of a half-dozen or so, cows and calves with perhaps one bull, and, of course, you see the bulls singly and in twos and threes as well. They really do like water. You often see them out on the flood plains, buried to their bellies in deep mud, grazing through the muck quite contentedly.

As big as they are, water buffalo are clearly formidable beasts, requiring powerful cartridges and well-constructed bullets. Like any wild bovine, they are unpredictable. Unprovoked charges probably aren't any more common than with African buffalo, but they do occur—and a wounded water buffalo is nothing to trifle with. That said, I have not found them to be as wary as African buffalo. This could be at least partly because they exist in a total absence of predators save man, and in the most remote areas, it is quite likely that most buffalo have never seen a human. You have to get the wind right, of course, but I haven't found them as difficult to stalk as African buffalo (this is aided by their generally smaller groups), and often they seem to have a curiosity that is totally lacking in African buffalo.

Steve and Dave and I hunted hard for several days without seeing any really big bulls, but we eventually found quite a reasonable bull grazing in a little ravine bordered by high grass. We made a quick stalk, expecting to take him from the bank above. Our approach was well concealed, so I don't know if he heard something or possibly caught a bit of scent—or perhaps it was just time for him to come up out of the draw. Whatever, we were just approaching the lip of the ravine when we saw movement in the grass right in front of us. He appeared at just a few yards, and as I gave him both barrels with the .470, he swapped ends and vanished just as quickly. He was down in the tall grass within twenty yards, but it was

My 2004 water buffalo was the kind of bull I'd been looking for. The horns go up rather than out, but the length is extreme and the bases are excellent. At least at this writing, there are plenty of great bulls like this in the most remote parts of Eastern Arnhem Land.

only when we approached him that I fully appreciated how big these things are.

Bigger and Better

Although it seemed we had traveled to Earth's end (and back again to get out of there), I had the impression that we were hunting remnant animals, evidenced by some abandoned campsites and corrals (many buffalo were rounded up and taken to market live). As is the case with Cape buffalo, it takes a long time, a decade and more, for a water buffalo bull to reach his maximum horn growth. Then it takes a few more years for him to wear down his horns and grow old. That first bull was all right and is the kind of bull most hunters take today. There are better, but you must penetrate even deeper into Outback.

Penfold understood this, and within a couple years he had it figured out. The next time I tried, he was hunting in far Eastern Arnhem Land, near the salt water of Blue Mud Bay, site of one of the last serious confrontations (not so long ago, in the 1930s), between the Australian government and the aborigines. These are buffalo that have never been market hunted and have never been culled. The only impact is very limited aboriginal hunting and some limited trophy hunting.

There are not vast numbers of buffalo. My own theory is that the buffalo, introduced a century and a half ago near the coast, are just now reaching this area. The great numbers that are now gone existed hundreds of miles to the west, so I think the buffalo along the eastern coast of Eastern Arnhem Land are still the advance guard of this great migration—except the bulk of the main herd was wiped out behind them. If this is correct, and if utilization remains at the same level it is now, then, in time, there will be many more buffalo in this remote corner of the Outback.

Right now, buffalo are plentiful there, if not crowded, and there are bulls that are big and old and heavy-horned. On that trip, in 1997, Chub Eastman and I took a light plane to a dirt strip near the coast, then drove just a half-hour to a little cluster of tents and shacks that served as our camp. Camps in the Outback—and I have now been in a half-dozen—look a lot like African camps, though a common eating area gets roofed with tin, rather than thatch, and sleeping tents are more likely to be nylon than canvas. The big difference is there is no staff, so it's more like a North American camp. There might be a cook, but there are no skinners, tent boys, water carriers, or drivers. We did have a generator-powered washing machine! The other big difference in the Outback is there is relatively little other game. There are a few wallabies and kangaroos, and you will see dingoes (protected on aboriginal lands), and the occasional wild hog (definitely not protected). That's about it, other than the buffalo and a few huge, saltwater crocodiles in the rivers and lagoons. None of this is either good or bad, it's just the way it is, and it is not the same as Africa. It means that your guide has a great deal more work to do, and it also means that despite the vast distance that must be covered to get there, the hunt has limited objectives and will be fairly short.

This time we cut it a bit too short! Chub was with me, and while we wanted to see this new buffalo country, we were both in a fizz to get to Cobourg and hunt banteng, something neither of us had done. It had been a very heavy and unusually late rainy season, and a lot of country was still inaccessible. Thank God for Mike Warne and his winches! Even the roads that were passable had some bad spots, so winching our way out of the muck was a frequent event.

We saw a lot of buffalo in spite of the mud. Chub drew first shot and took a real whopper right out on the edge of a flood plain, literally slamming it to the ground with the .416 Weatherby he was using. Once again, the winch proved invaluable! We were able to drive the truck to the edge of the muck and snake the bull right out.

A day later, after passing up several more bulls, I made a mistake. I guess. We were headed back to camp just at sunset, and off to the left, in some thick eucalyptus, was a good-size herd of buffalo, maybe a dozen. The bull was over on the right-hand side, Lord, a sweeper. The left horn came out and swept back forever, the kind of buffalo you see in the old books. I was shooting

Water buffalo seem to me to be a bit more curious than African buffalo, possibly because they live in total absence of predators. It isn't uncommon for animals encountered in the bush to give you a look like this, not exactly like you owe him money, more like, "What in the world are you?"

a scoped Krieghoff double in .500-416. The bull was almost facing, just quartering slightly to me. I shot him right on the point of the shoulder. He rocked back on his heels as if to go down, then whirled to run. I shot him again quartering away, and he went down in just a few steps. Perfect. Except that I had failed to notice that a third of his left horn was broken off. Well, that left us plenty of time to hunt banteng.

Cobourg

The Cobourg Peninsula is remote today. I can't even imagine how remote it was when it was established as an outpost nearly two centuries ago! It is a uniquely beautiful area, pristine beaches surrounding much more lush vegetation than I have seen elsewhere in the Northern Territories. The camp there was another neat line of tents in earshot of the pounding surf, and the dining area looked out over a rocky surf line. The banteng, originally introduced as a meat source, are quite plentiful, but difficult to hunt in the thick cover they love. Sambar were also introduced, but they are not plentiful and seem more like ghosts. You find the occasional track or perhaps a shed antler, but the several dozen annual banteng hunters only take one or two sambar stags.

The banteng is a fairly small wild ox weighing perhaps eight hundred pounds, with simple, smooth horns that vary quite a bit in how they curve out from the head. They are thought to be the ancestors of at least some breeds of domestic cattle, and they certainly look it. Cows and young bulls tend to be tan in color, but the breeding bulls appear glossy black and are quite spectacular. As they get older, the color seems to fade, with very old bulls much more brown than black. What they lack in size they make up for in nasty temperament. Banteng are much more aggressive than water buffalo and may be more aggressive than African buffalo.

The Cobourg Peninsula, where Australia's banteng are found, has much denser cover than most of the Outback. This is jungle hunting, and in this close cover, the banteng are more aggressive than the much larger buffalo.

A very old banteng bull, taken with a Krieghoff .500-416 double. Banteng horns vary considerably, and older bulls are generally this brownish tan color, while younger breeding bulls are nearly black.

Charges are relatively common, and great caution is taken when approaching wounded animals. This may well be a result of the closer cover, just as African forest buffalo are thought to be more aggressive than their southern cousins.

Finding banteng is not difficult, but closing with them in the thick cover and getting a shot is much harder. They seem to occur in small family groups, much like the water buffalo, but only rarely do you catch them in the open. Mine was a very old bull walking alone. We spotted him from a little track and closed for a shot, and I didn't hit him as well as I should have. We followed for a couple of hundred yards, spotted him standing in some thick vegetation, and that was that. Chub's was also a very old bull on his own. We spotted him crossing a road well ahead of us, and when we closed on him, Chub did a much better job than I did, dropping him with one shot.

That hunt was really a bit too quick, and we left without me believing I had learned a great deal about banteng. The breeding bulls are truly striking, and the Cobourg itself is beautiful. I suspect I'll find myself there again one of these days.

Big Buffalo at Last

Although I enjoy the Outback immensely, the South Pacific is a big place, and there are some other things I wanted to hunt. So I hadn't given a lot of thought to trying to find a really big buffalo "just once more." Sometimes these things just happen. Penfold kept telling me that he was finding better and better buffalo. My daughter, Brittany, had suddenly taken an interest in hunting at the advanced age of seventeen, and we'd recently completed a wonderful plains-game hunt in Namibia. Now eighteen, she was bugging me to hunt in Australia. Why not? I figured I wouldn't see the kind of water buffalo I wanted, but I figured she'd be a whole lot less picky and we'd have a great time. We went in late June 2004. This is a perfect time in the Northern Territories, not only cooler "winter" weather, but late enough so that most of the

We lost a herd of banteng in thick vegetation and hiked on out to the beach. The Cobourg is uniquely beautiful, with thick forest surrounded by pristine beaches and pounding surf. It's a great hunt.

waters from the rains will have receded, and so almost all roads will be passable.

We spent a couple of days "warming up" on wild hogs at Penfold's camp on Dorisvale Station, not far from Katherine. Earlier, I mentioned that we took a Ruger No. 1 in .405 Winchester, and I was grateful for the opportunity to see how the bullets performed on hogs before we tried it out on something as large as a water buffalo. The 300-grain Hornady bullets, although too light for the caliber for my taste, penetrated deeply and performed wonderfully. I figured they would work just fine, and in any case, I planned to be at Brittany's shoulder with one of the Mauser-actioned .458's Penfold keeps in camp. Brittany and I took really super hogs, and in addition to me having confidence in the cartridge, she now had confidence in the rifle.

I had expected to fly from Dorisvale to Eastern Arnhem Land, so I was horrified when the planned charter fell through. I thought I knew what we were in for, and I didn't even tell Brittany how bad it would be. Good thing I didn't. As before, we did some shopping in Katherine and pulled out in the late morning. Although the distance is much greater, the roads to this area were a whole lot better. By dusk, we were well into aboriginal territory, and the only thing that slowed us down was the water buffalo we started seeing along the road. We pulled into camp at 10 P.M., a long run, but nothing like what I'd been through a decade before.

We slept in that first morning, heading out for a little recce in the early afternoon. It was too easy, really. Just a few kilometers from camp, we ran into a small group of buffalo feeding in some heavy brush off to the left. We stopped and looked, not expecting much—and I nearly dropped my binocular when the bull stepped out from behind one of his cows. He was huge-bodied, standing a foot taller than the cows. And he had horns to match. They were incredibly massive all the way to the tips, and he was one of those wide, flat, impressive bulls—a sweeper. I had not seen a water buffalo this good before, so no way were we going to pass him up.

We got within about forty yards and got Brittany set up on a shooting stick, but there was just too much brush, and he was

My daughter Brittany and I pose with her magnificent buffalo. The horn tips are worn, reducing the score, but the mass is incredible and the spread tremendous. This was a huge-bodied bull as well. I'm sure he weighed 2,500 pounds, a totally impossible weight for any African buffalo.

moving around, feeding. He stood clear for maybe an instant, then the moment passed, and he moved farther into the cover to join three or four cows. We started to move to the left, but there was another cow there with a tiny calf. Stuck. We could still see just the outline of the bull, and then he turned and started walking toward us. We all dropped, and guide Peter Harding got in front of Brittany and had her rest the rifle over his shoulder, whispering to me, "You tell her when to shoot."

My guess is the bull saw something when we were set up on him, and now he was coming back to check it out. He was not aggressive, but he was moving steadily straight to us, head down, with slow and steady strides. A brain shot was possible, but Brittany and I had never talked about that—and, quite frankly, I wouldn't have taken it myself. Sooner or later he would open up a bit of shoulder.

When he was about twenty-five yards, Brittany whispered, "Daddy, he's getting closer." I glanced at her; her eyes were wide but the rifle was steady. I just nodded.

At fifteen yards, she whispered again, "Daddy, he's really close." Tell me something I don't know. I had moved the .458 up so all I needed to do was lift it up and fire. "Just wait," I whispered back. I was thinking, "Three more steps."

Twelve yards in front of us, directly between the buffalo and us, was one fairly stout little sapling. I figured the buffalo would have to turn one way or the other when he reached it. He turned to our right, his left, and as he came around the little tree he lifted his head slightly.

"Shoot him on the point of the shoulder, just under the horn," I whispered. The little rifle cracked almost instantly, and I saw dust fly on the exact spot I was looking at. The buffalo rocked back hard, and I thought he was going down. Then he gathered himself and ran back toward the cows, but not well. I was standing ready with the .458, but it wasn't needed. We lost sight of him, but I was certain he had gone down among the cows. We approached carefully and saw several cows leave, but no bull. Then we saw the black, horizontal mass close to the ground, and Peter had Brittany shoot one more time. No movement at all. He was finished.

In body, this was the largest water buffalo I have ever seen. No Cape buffalo could match him, and I wouldn't be surprised if he weighed as much as twenty-five hundred pounds. The horns were long and incredibly heavy, a great trophy—and a whole lot better than any water buffalo I had ever shot! Brittany was thrilled, Dad was thrilled, and I didn't really need one.

I found one anyway. Peter and I turned down several pretty darned good bulls, and we were heading back toward camp (again, but this time it was a warm midday), when we saw a bull standing alone in open forest. This one required no discussion. I got out and moved in behind some trees. He was maybe sixty yards away, and I shot him at about the same angle as Brittany's shot. He took the bullet just as hard, then turned and wove off through the forest. It was open enough that I could run with him, stuffing another shell into the single shot. When he turned a bit, I shot him again, and this time he went down. Then he was up again, shot again, and down again, and we walked up to a really magnificent Asian water buffalo.

A Perfect Buffalo Hunt
Chapter 15

A s I was planning this volume devoted to the great black buffalo that I love so well, it always seemed to me that I should finish it with an account of a most memorable, most ideal, most *perfect* buffalo hunt. But which one? I've had more than twenty-five years of African hunting, more than fifty safaris. Buffalo hunting has not been a part of all of these, no more than all buffalo hunts have been successful. But the safaris where no time was devoted to buffalo are in the minority, and the only reason I didn't hunt buffalo on them was because there were no buffalo in the area.

The "best" buffalo hunt? There haven't been any bad ones, although I haven't loved them all, especially not at the time. Some have been painful, but those dished out hard lessons I badly needed. There are some mistakes I've made over and over and will keep on making—but others have required just one lesson! I cannot give you a best buffalo hunt, because they have all been wonderful. I think my most recent buffalo hunt, in July and August 2004, was one of the best. I have often referred to it in this volume, partly because it was the freshest in my mind, partly because it was so perfect, and largely because, for the first time in my African hunting career, I was able to devote a full two weeks to doing nothing but hunt buffalo. I did this in the company of a true expert, Andrew Dawson, and I learned things that I did not know I didn't know.

But for the most memorable buffalo hunt of all, I can reach back through the years, and although I knew I wanted to end this book with that hunt, I was halfway through with the writing of it before I knew exactly which hunt it should be. Certain elements were necessary. It needed to be a hunt that yielded a really good bull, not because I'm a trophy freak, but because I revere big buffalo and have spent so much time in their pursuit. And as much as I love that buffalo, it could not be the hunt in Mto Wa Mbu that yielded my very best bull: That bull was a pure gift, not an animal we had worked for (and if I hadn't looked the gift horse in the mouth I would have taken an even bigger bull). No, the most memorable had to be a tough hunt, a difficult hunt, and an animal I had in some measure earned.

The most memorable hunt needed excitement, because excitement is part and parcel to buffalo hunting. (Come to think of it, I can't think of any buffalo hunt that hasn't been exciting, but some have sparked more of an adrenaline rush than others.) It also needed to be a hunt that incorporated a strong chance for failure, because that, too, after hours on the tracks, is part and parcel to buffalo hunting. Finally, purely for me because I care about such things, it needed to be a hunt that ended with a most memorable shot.

Zambia, 1996

I have written about this safari before, and I suppose I will write about it again, because it was a very special, bittersweet time. Robert E. Petersen of Petersen Publishing—some call him "Pete," others call him "Bob," and some in the shop called him "chief," but to me he was, and still is, "Mr. Petersen"—was just concluding the sale of the publishing company I had called home for seventeen years, other than the Marine Corps, the only real job I've ever had. I had no idea what the future might hold. That was seven years ago, and I'm still writing for the magazines that used to be part of the Petersen group, so I guess it worked out OK. But I didn't know that then. I received no bonus, no golden parachute, no guarantee of future employment, nor did I expect anything. Indeed, quite unexpectedly, I got something far more precious that I will always be grateful for.

I took this wonderful sitatunga on the first day of the safari. It didn't seem that things could get better, but they did, each and every day!

Mr. Petersen gathered up a chosen few—his right-hand man, Ken Elliott, his ranch manager, Gary Williams, his longtime friend, the great artist Doug Van Howd, and me—and in late September of 1996, we climbed into his Gulfstream and flew to Zambia for a safari with Russ Broom, first spending a few days in the Bangweulu, then the Mulobezi block near the Kafue National Park. Although we had done some bird hunting, it was the first time I had ever been on a big-game hunt with "the chief." Come to think of it, and despite what many of you think, in the now twenty-five years I have written for the magazines Bob Petersen created, this was the first and so far the only time I have been to Africa on a "company hunt."

It started out a bit rocky. I was driving from my home in Paso Robles to the Van Nuys airport, about one hundred eighty miles. With about fifty miles to go, I stopped at the rest area in Tejon Pass to answer an urgent call of nature. When I returned to my Blazer, I managed to notice a massive pool of oil spreading under the car. Not having much choice, I drove to the closest service station, about three miles away. My gun case, duffel, and I were delivered to the Petersen Aviation terminal in Van Nuys by tow truck, while my Blazer, with a bad seal, was delivered to a garage where it sat until I got back!

From there it got better. We overnighted in Puerto Rico, refueled in Recife, Brazil, and again in Ivory Coast, touching down in Lusaka in the midmorning. By three in the afternoon, we were in Bangweulu. Mr. Petersen and I had the only sitatunga licenses, so we were asked if we wanted to sit in machans (the African tree stand) that afternoon. Dumb question! We threw our duffels in our huts and dug out ammo and binoculars and such, stopping on the way to check zero on a cardboard box.

They wanted to use two machans, one fairly close to the edge of the swamp and the other about a half-mile walk through the papyrus. Mr. Petersen had a bad knee, swollen like a grapefruit and worrying all of us. He opted for the close blind, visible from mine far off across a sea of papyrus. At least for a short time. I hadn't been in the blind for a half-hour, when the most marvelous sitatunga bull I have ever seen stepped out of the

Robert E. "Pete" Petersen relaxing around the fire circle in our first camp in Zambia, the Lake Bangweulu "common" camp shared by most hunting parties in this area.

swamp in front of me. I shot him, and we worked our way through the muck to him.

Only then did it occur to me what I had done. For seventeen years it had been an article of faith that, no matter what, if you go hunting with the chief, you never, *ever* shoot a larger animal than his. No matter what. One look at this sitatunga, and I knew nobody on this safari was going to shoot a bigger one. By now it was getting dark, and I would be compounding my crime by keeping the chairman of the board waiting in the dark in the middle of the Bangweulu Swamp.

Well, no point in shooting myself now. We carried the sitatunga out through the swamp, reaching the vehicle about a half-hour after full dark. And there was Robert E. Petersen, camera in hand, a day from his seventieth birthday, waiting in the dark to see the sitatunga. "Turn it a bit more," he said, as he lay in the cold mud taking pictures. Like all of us, I'd bought into the myth without ever knowing the man.

Pete Petersen outside his hut in Russ Broom's Kafue camp. Typical camps in Zambia use a cement floor and thatched walls and roof, comfortable and easy to maintain.

Zambian PH Austin Wienand and Pete Petersen with a nice black lechwe. This was Pete's seventieth birthday, celebrated with a cake in camp.

We celebrated his birthday in camp in Bangweulu, a fine place for such a milestone, and then we flew to the Mulobezi. Mr. Petersen didn't get a sitatunga. He turned down several, seeing nothing that he wanted, and I don't think that bothered him at all.

Mulobezi

Except for Pete's sitatunga, we filled all of our licenses in Bangweulu, but that was nothing like the luck we had in Mulobezi. Russ Broom, our outfitter, personally guided Mr. Petersen. I hunted with Angie Angelloz, an extremely talented, young Zimbabwe hunter who, most regrettably, has since decided on a more stable career. Austin Wienand, a veteran Zambian hunter, guided Ken Elliott. Doug Van Howd wasn't hunting, and Gary Williams sort of pinch-hit with all of us.

Earlier, I told about the great luck that I had, taking eland on the first day and roan near the end. Everyone had a similar story.

Pete shot a fine eland and a monstrous sable, and also a great roan on the last day. Ken got a beautiful leopard right off the bat, and a good sable, as well. Gary, on his first African hunt, shot a fifty-eight-inch kudu. For the first few days, however, buffalo were a bit of a problem. The rains had lasted late, leaving more water in the park than usual. The buffalo were starting to come in, but we were impatient. With little else on our plate—certainly nothing more important—Angie and I scratched around for buffalo, tracking a few *dugga* boys without success. After several days, it was clear the buffalo simply weren't there yet. Being a bit of a pessimist, I had doubts about any of us getting decent buffalo. I needn't have worried.

It was happening while we watched. We'd been there maybe six days when Ken shot the first buffalo, a wonderful bull with a forty-three-inch spread. I think, although I'm not certain, this is his best buffalo to this day. One morning, Gary Williams was with us when we spotted a good-size herd feeding slowly straight for the park. We followed quickly on foot, and long

On this last day, Pete Petersen was still out hunting, getting his roan. Gary Williams, Ken Elliott, and I show our stunning results of something close to twelve hunting days. It's not likely we'll ever be this lucky again.

Pete Petersen took a number of really fine trophies, including a good roan on the very last day. But this incredible sable was probably his best, the finest sable I have personally ever seen.

before they reached sanctuary, Gary took a nice bull. I was happy for him—truly, I've shot plenty of buffalo—but at this point, they were still scarce enough I couldn't help but think that I probably wouldn't get one. I think I got mine a couple of days later, and Pete got his buffalo last. We were all worried about him tracking buffalo on that bad knee, but when the time came, he ignored it. He got to the buffalo, and he shot it well with his famous old .460 G&A, another really superb bull, not quite as wide, but with a spectacular curl to the horns. Among three hunters, the only license we didn't fill in that incredible ten days was Pete's lion. He and Russ hunted hard and turned down some young males, but that was the one thing our great hunting team couldn't make happen.

A Wonderful Buffalo

It was a little late in the morning when we picked up the tracks of a bachelor herd. We figured the group to be about seven bulls. They were morning tracks, which was good. But the spoor led straight toward the park, which was very bad; it was already

I was also charmed throughout the trip. We messed up and I didn't have the leopard license I expected, so this magnificent Livingstone eland was sort of a consolation prize—and a darned good one at that!

late, and the boundary was not a long distance away. Angie figured they might stop short of the boundary, and in any case, we had to try. These were the first buffalo tracks we had cut since Gary's buffalo.

The bulls led us straight as an arrow for several miles, not stopping to feed, not meandering, just cooking along straight for sanctuary. It looked really bad, especially since the park couldn't be more than a mile or two away now. But the tracks were still fresh, and we were committed. Besides, it was nearly eleven o'clock now, well into the heat of the day, and there was absolutely nothing else to do.

We almost ran into them. It was relatively open *miombo* forest, and with almost none of the typical meandering of their tracks, they had stopped short and were feeding. We got ourselves stopped without spooking them, and the trackers evaluated the wind. It was hot now, and the breezes were becoming unstable. We shifted far to the right and came in from a different angle, slowly and carefully. There was one bull plainly visible, and beyond him we could just see hints of black that had to be buffalo.

We made an ant heap, but still couldn't see anything more. As we watched, the closest buffalo lay down. What bad luck! We looked for a while, but the wind was really tricky now, and the buffalo seemed to be bedded tight.

The right thing was to back off and wait, and this is what we did. We didn't wait all that long, but it seemed an eternity, sitting or lying on baked earth in scanty shade. Every few minutes we would check on the one buffalo we could see. He was lying on his brisket, legs folded, chewing his cud and obviously quite content. We still had no clue what might be in the herd. The bull we could see was mature, but very average. As for the rest, there was surely something good among this many bulls. But would we ever see them?

We talked about moving this way and that, but the winds were all over the place, so this was mostly talk. At one point, Angie and I advanced a hundred yards to a big tree, but the wind was just no good. If we pushed it, we would spook them, and all would be for

On any given day, we had three hunting vehicles out in Russ Broom's Mulobezi area. Encounters with other members of our group weren't common, but when they happened, we'd stop and visit for a few minutes, then continue the hunt.

naught. We retreated; all we could really do was wait them out and hope things got better.

After a hundred eternities of heat and mopane bees, the one bull we could see got up and wandered off through scattered trees. Now we could see a couple more buffalo in the distance. They were all up. All right. Now how is the wind? Still not very good, but maybe steadier.

We moved on them, Angie crawling forward with me, while Gary and the trackers held their ground. We made the shelter of that same big tree and could see them up ahead, feeding away in a grassy swale. It looked like they were all mature bulls, rare to see so many together. We were much too far to shoot, and it was far too thick to be sure what was there, but so far so good. There was plenty of cover, and they were feeding slowly, so all we had to do was slip out to one side, then come in on them.

This thought hadn't even been spoken when the buffalo, all of them at once, suddenly spooked and stampeded straight away. Hell! The wind had seemed a bit better, but they must have caught a stray eddy of our scent. Angie and I stood under the shelter of the big tree and watched the dust as they vanished into the trees. The park was too close, so I figured that was the end of that. *This* thought hadn't even been spoken, nor had the dust started to settle, when they came stampeding right back.

They were coming straight at us, and for the first time, in rapid-fire arithmetic, we could see they were nine bulls. They ran in tight, echelon formation, the lead bull on our right, the rear bull on our left, the other seven in between, all running at full speed straight to us. All nine were fully mature, grownup bulls, some clearly bigger than others—but there wasn't much time to sort through them. It reminded me of one of Douglas Van Howd's paintings. At the time I had hunted buffalo for twenty years, and it was the most awesome sight I had ever seen. It remains so to this day.

As they bore down on us, Angie and I left the shelter of our tree and stepped forward to meet them. This may not have been the smartest move in the world, but it would be a running shot. We needed to be completely clear of the tree, and I wanted that

Of course, the point to all this is that it was a perfect buffalo hunt. The safari was much more than that, which helped make it so perfect, and a buffalo this perfect didn't hurt. The PH is Zimbabwean Angie Angelloz, a truly great young hunter. Without his cool nerves and quick thinking, we would have shot a lesser bull.

shot to be as close as possible. They saw us, of course, but they were as committed as we were and held their course. We were almost in front of the trailing edge of the echelon, so close the lead bull would pass at a couple of dozen yards. The rear bulls might just miss us.

I was focused on the lead bull, an exceptional buffalo with wide, heavy horns. He was also in the tight pack the easiest to shoot. I was bringing the rifle up when Angie, one of the coolest customers I ever hunted with, said flatly, calmly, with total confidence and with no room for argument, "Shoot the second one."

He was dead right. I should have seen it, but I was concentrating on the lead bull and the easier shot. The second bull was even wider, *impossibly* wide with a wonderful curl. I put the rifle up and started to swing with him, but now I had to hurry. Bulls to the rear were starting to catch up, breaking that clean echelon, and in a few strides that fine second bull would be masked. I got the big double up and swung with him as if he were a big, black quail, focusing on shooting him just under the curve of the horn exactly as Geoff Broom had taught me.

This bull was probably forty yards away. After the shot, the remainder thundered past, the rear bulls almost close enough to touch. But that bull went nowhere. The 500-grain Woodleigh entered just under the curve of the horn where the neck joins the shoulder. The head snapped back, all four feet folded in mid-gallop, and he crashed down hard and slid forward, adding more dust as the rest of the group galloped past. I shot him with the second barrel as soon as they cleared, but that second shot wasn't as good. Nor was it necessary. He was down and done. A little flat and with very average bosses, he was nearly forty-seven inches wide—easily the second-best buffalo I have ever shot, but by far the most spectacular finish to any buffalo hunt, and a golden memory of a most remarkable safari.